IN THE GREAT TOGETHER

IN THE GREAT TOGETHER

One-Act Plays

Seth Alan Barkas

Hannacroix Creek Books, Inc.
Stamford, CT

This book is dedicated by the editor and publisher to the talent and the memory of her brother, Seth Alan Barkas (1945-1969)

Published by:
Hannacroix Creek Books, Inc.
1127 High Ridge Road, PMB #110
Stamford, CT 06905-1203
Phone (203) 321-8674 Fax (203) 968-0193
e-mail: hannacroix@aol.com
www.hannacroixcreekbooks.com

LCCN: 97-073497

ISBN: 1-889262-07-2 (hardcover)
ISBN: 1-889262-51-X (trade paperback)

Thanks to Ken Iglehart of *Baltimore* magazine for granting permission to reprint the tribute to Seth Alan Barkas, published in the March 1969 issue of *Baltimore* magazine, included at the end of About the Author.

Contents

Editor's Note

The publication of *In the Great Together: One Act Plays* fulfills a promise I made to my late brother: that I would find a way to share his literary accomplishments with the world—not just the tragedy of his death at the age of twenty-three from the stab wounds inflicted by a gang of youths during a robbery.

This is an incredibly difficult editor's note for me to write without breaking down into tears and sadness. It is difficult enough to lose a sibling, especially in the formative years, but the way my brother died just heightened the devastation and loss that everyone who knew and loved my brother felt. At the time of my brother's death, he had been married for three years to a talented artist, Karen, and he had been raising her five-year-old son from her first marriage as his own. They were expecting another child in a few months; that son was born two months after my brother's death.

I was so impacted by what happened to my brother, as well as perplexed by the criminal justice system, that I spent almost a decade researching crime, violence, getting a masters in criminal justice, teaching criminology, working with crime victims, and writing my book, *Victims*, which was published by Charles Scribner's Sons in 1978. I went on to obtain a doctorate in sociology; crime and deviance was one of my three areas of specialization. (I recently learned from my older sister that our brother's murder impacted on her career path as well. It was a key motivation in her decision to become a professional mediator as a way of helping others to non-violently resolve disputes.)

In the preface to my book *Victims*, I wrote about what happened to my brother, and the impact his murder had on our family. But I have always wanted to honor my brother's talent as a playwright and writer rather than focusing on his violent death and crime victim status. At the time of his death, he was a freelance film critic for *Baltimore* magazine as well as a theatre critic for *Show Business* newspaper. (It was after he had seen a play that he was planning to review that he was accosted by the muggers who stabbed him.)

We immediately after his death established a memorial fund and scholarship in his name at his alma mater, New York University, a creative writing award that is given out each year to a student whose literary work wins in the annual competition. Although through this scholarship we have been honoring my late brother's name and his commitment to creativity and literature, the scholarship honored the writing of others.

Yet for years following my brother's death I was too numbed by his loss to think about what I could do to honor his talent. I was even unaware of the completed dramatic works that are in this collection until the mid-1990s, almost thirty years after his death, when my sister-in-law gave me a big box of files of his writings. Initially I could not bring myself to look through those files. But when I finally did, and I read the four plays that are gathered together in this collection for the first time, I was astounded and impressed by the maturity and insightfulness of my late brother's writings. (I tried to read the plays as objectively as possible, not as the sister of the late playwright, but relying on my professional and educational credentials as a freelance theatre critic for *Back Stage* newspaper for seven years as well as someone who has studied dramatic literature and acting in college, who is a member of The Dramatists Guild, and who has written several plays herself.)

Once I decided I had to find a way to publish my brother's four one-act plays, with the hope that the plays will also be produced, the laborious process began, in the days before scanners were very accurate, of scanning my brother's original typed manuscripts into computer files that could be formatted for publication. Since I could not consult the author if I had any questions about a word or even about spelling, I made the decision to adhere to Seth's exact manuscripts, adding his handwritten notes if it looked as if it was my late brother's intent to include that additional line of dialogue, or direction, to the typed master play. The only changes I have made were because of grammatical, typographical, or spelling errors.

Finally, after many years working on these plays in my spare time, and after the additional final proofreading of Texas-based Peggy Stautberg, I am able to share my brother's plays with the world.

There are some people who are granted longevity but squander those years or feel frustrated that they have never achieved the creative contributions they had hoped to leave behind whether that is in fiction, nonfiction, drama, poetry, art, music, or dance. There are others, like my brother, who live relatively short lives but they leave behind creative contributions that can grant them creative immortality (as well as the legacy of his two sons and their children).

I hope you enjoy reading these plays as much as I have each and every time I have read each one. Considering the fact that these plays were written in the mid-to-late 1960s, they stand up amazingly well. Of course there may be some references that seem a bit dated but that should not diminish the worth of these unique one-act plays.

Each one-act play is distinctive in subject matter and style. The first play in the collection is *Maximilan.* It takes place in 1867 in a makeshift prison cell the night before the execution of 35-year-old Emperor Maximilian of Mexico, who was sent to rule Mexico from his native Austria by Emperor Napoleon of France. A young aristocrat, Constantine, is smuggled into the prison disguised as a stable boy to try to talk Maximilian into leaving his adopted country of Mexico, rather than be executed. Maximilian explains: "Can't you understand that I can't leave my country?" to which Constantine replies, "Do you think it is any easier to leave a friend?"

The second play is *Cry of the Boy*, a more existential drama that delves into the everyday life of a 17-year-old boy and his relationship with his mother and father.

The Devil and Don Quijote, the third play in this collection by Seth Alan Barkas, is a fascinating application of the classic Cervantes tale to the story of Don Quijote, a man who has just escaped from an old age home and who wears a homemade suite of armor with a pot as a helmet.

Scorpio, the fourth and final play in this collection of one-act plays, explores the relationship between a 20-year-old woman named Tom, and Stanley, a 19-year-old who wanders into Tom's apartment as he was going door to door in a Bronx apartment building, selling merchandise made by the blind. In this two-character play, Tom and Stanley explore through their chance encounter their contrasting childhoods and personalities.

Plays are meant to be performed and these plays are no exceptions. If you or your amateur troupe, school, community, or professional production company wish to perform any of these plays, just contact our publishing company (hannacroix@aol.com) to work out the details. (The first performance of each of the plays will be credited with being the world premiere of that play.)

I chose the title for this collection of one-act plays by my late brother from a line in the very powerful and prophetic poem that he wrote just a few weeks before his death. That poem was published in an anthology of poetry entitled, *The Healing Power of Creative Mourning: Poems* (Hannacroix Creek Books, Inc., 2000), available through local or online bookstores or your local library. Here are the last lines from Seth's untitled poem, including the phrase, "in the great together":

> In the woods of our youth,
> he was discovered,
> dead at 24 years, with an
> overdose of heroin. It happened;
> jumbling my memories. I'm
> not sure he was a "good"
> person, but I liked him. He
> was good to me. And whether I
> liked him or not, it's unimportant.
> Sooner or later I'm going to join
> him in the great together.
> It scares me.

My late brother's family will be given his (the author's) share of any income that this book generates, whether from book sales, foreign or movie rights, or performance fees. The publishing company also plans to donate from its share of the book's earnings to the New York University scholarship established in Seth's name, the Seth Barkas Memorial Prize in Creative Writing.

Thank you for reading these plays. If you are in the theatre world as an actor, actress, director, producer, or critic, we appreciate you getting the word out that these four plays are available for production.

Although personal replies are not guaranteed, I certainly welcome your comments and, if deemed appropriate, will gladly send along your communications or feedback to my late brother's family on your behalf.

Jan Yager, Ph.D.
[the former J.L. (Janet) Barkas]
Editor, *In the Great Together*
c/o Hannacroix Creek Books, Inc.
1127 High Ridge Road, #110
Stamford, CT 06905 USA
hannacroix@aol.com
www.hannacroixcreekbooks.com

Maximilian

Maximilian

SETTING: *A dank wine cellar in a Mexican ranch that has been hastily converted into sleeping accommodations for the imprisoned Emperor Maximilian. The cellar is filled with wine racks that give the illusion that the room is like a maze. A small table is in the center of the cellar and a cot is underneath a high, minuscule window.*

TIME: *The night before the execution of the Emperor Maximilian in 1867.*

CHARACTERS:

Maximilian, former Emperor of Mexico
Rolpo
Constantine
Benito Juarez
General Lopez

AT RISE: *Maximilian, a tall, bearded man of 35 who has an aristocratic stature and wears Austrian clothing with Mexican ornamentation, is sleeping on the cot under the window. He is feverishly tossing his covers as he dreams of his execution and the audience hears the sounds of muffled drums; a soldier shouting the commands of execution; and a volley of rifle shots exploding. At this point, Maximilian raises himself from his cot and we hear a tapping at the door of the wine cellar.*

MAXIMILIAN: *(Stirring from sleep)* My God, what an awful nightmare. I must make a note of it in my diary...Wait...There's someone there.

ROLPO: *(In the heavy voice of an enormously fat man. Rolpo is a huge man with flabby cheeks, a slovenly example of the Army of the People's Democracy.)*

Excuse me, your exalted Kingship.

MAXIMILIAN: Oh.*(A sigh of relief)* It's only the jailer. That's you, isn't it, Rolpo?

ROLPO: It most certainly is, your exalted Kingship.

Editor's note: Napoleon III, who was trying to create a Mexican empire, persuaded Ferdinand Maximilan (1832-67), the Austrian archduke, to become Emperor of Mexico (1864-67), bringing along his wife Carlotta, a princess, daughter of Leopold I of Belgium. However, from his arrival in Mexico, he discovered that the country was loyal to Benito Juarez. Napoleon withdrew his troops and Juarez gained control. Maxmilian was condemned to death. This play is the fictitious account of an attempt to talk Maximilan into abdicating his throne and avoiding his death by a firing squad.

MAXIMILIAN: I am the Imperial Emperor and while I am the guest in this most charming establishment, I wish to be left alone to sleep.

ROLPO: Could I have some wine?

MAXIMILIAN: *(Standing on his cot, ranting)* Why you garlic-breathed baboon. I was having the most exquisite dream of sugar plums and...

ROLPO: *He* said you would give me wine.

MAXIMILIAN: Who? *(He goes toward his table to light the lamp)*

VOICE: *(From behind the door)* Maximilian.

MAXIMILIAN: *(Just as he lights a match)* Constantine...Well, bring him in, Rolpo, if you want your wine, my fine good-natured—garlic-breathed—jailer.
(*He lights the lamp as the door opens and Rolpo and Constantine enter. Constantine is a frail, 17-year-old youth, of aristocratic breeding, who is disguised as a stable hand. As soon as Maximilian spies Constantine, they embrace).*

MAXIMILIAN: *(Glancing toward Rolpo)* You can go now...Don't worry, dear Rolpo. This is my stable lad. We formerly rode together. You ride, don't you?

ROLPO: There's some that ride...And then, there's some that don't ride.

MAXIMILIAN: And you?

ROLPO: I walk *(holding his belly).* It comes natural to me...Your lad here said you'd be willing to give me some of this wine. That's what he said to me, he did.

MAXIMILIAN: And so I will. *(He walks over to Rolpo)*
Your choice of wines and we will all drink our bellies full when I'm warm.

ROLPO: *(Eagerly scooping up an armful of bottles.)*
There's many an hour of warmth in these.

MAXIMILIAN: But I need a blanket.

CONSTANTINE: Do be a kind gentleman and fetch my master his blanket...he'll catch his death in this damp place.

ROLPO: Can't see that it makes much difference. They're going to shoot him in the morning anyway.

MAXIMILIAN: All the more reason that I be healthy for the execution. It's not respectable to shoot a man who is too weak to stand up. Now the blanket and later some wine.

ROLPO: *(Replacing the wine bottles)* I'll find you a nice warm blanket but you'd better keep a close watch on your visitor there. He looks suspiss... suspiss...

CONSTANTINE: Suspicious?

ROLPO: That's just what I said. Suspiss... Suspiss...
(He exits)

CONSTANTINE: *(He grasps Maximilian's arm)* What a foolish oaf but tonight you'll have no need to worry about him.

MAXIMILIAN: Tonight, tonight...I must finish my book of etiquette, which will also serve as the diary of my life. Why are you here, Constantine?

CONSTANTINE: Are you not glad to see me?

MAXIMILIAN: My orders were that no one should attempt to see me. The price for an aristocrat's blood is high these days. And what if you had been caught?

CONSTANTINE: To serve my Emperor, I would risk capture, anything.

MAXIMILIAN: Oh, my dear, wonderful boy. How noble you are. Do you know what would happen if you were caught? They would want to house you in here with me. There's barely enough air for one. The two of us would suffocate. Confining a man with breeding to a hovel like this is a horrible torture.

CONSTANTINE: But Maximilian. I've come to take you from this torture. Napoleon has...

MAXIMILIAN: Now, you've brought up an interesting subject. My faithful, Louis the Magnificent, Louis the Incorruptible...oh, he has so many titles...
(He thumbs through his book of etiquette)
This book will one day serve as a guide...But about Louis...The Majestic Emperor of France, Sovereign Prince of Spain and the

Protector of the German State...I feel naked in his wake...

CONSTANTINE: If you'll listen to me...

MAXIMILIAN: Louis has more titles than the last king of the Holy Roman Empire. For a man without a drop of royal blood, this general has managed to convert himself into a noble. Juarez? He's an honest man. A general, but has he made himself king because he has won a war? No. In this hemisphere they become presidents. That deserves a footnote.

CONSTANTINE: I've been hiding under the floorboards of a shed for the past four days—since our defeat—all I could think about was you, how to free you from this trap.

MAXIMILIAN: Enough. Make yourself ready to sneak out of this place the way you came in. As a stable lad. Away and forget me.

CONSTANTINE: I will not leave and I will not forget you.

MAXIMILIAN: And forget me to my wife, Carlotta. I fear she has already forgotten me on her own.

CONSTANTINE: Everything is not lost. The French...

MAXIMILIAN: Are not sending troops.

CONSTANTINE: He regrets...

MAXIMILIAN: That due to circumstances beyond the control of the Incorruptible's hand, he cannot aid his dear ally in Mexico, whom he has betrayed three times in the past five years. And that his Venerable Sovereign Princeliness sends his most sincere regrets.

CONSTANTINE: In a few hours we can be free of here. The damp has gotten to you. Are you ill? Yes. *(Maximilian stands on top of his cot and gazes through his window)* Yes, he is ill.

MAXIMILIAN: I would ride with Carlotta through the country; visiting our people. Singing songs with them. They are an easy people. With their glistening white clothes—looking like village saints. The stars here, they say, can be talked to. When they answer your wishes, they twinkle.

CONSTANTINE: Maximilian, you aren't well. Let me take you home.

MAXIMILIAN: To Europe? To Austria? Where there are no men with somber smiles leading burros into fields? This is a rich land and this is my home.

CONSTANTINE: There's not much time. In Austria we have friends. We can raise another army. This can be our country once again.

MAXIMILIAN: Ah, sweet, generous Constantine. Our country again. If only it ever was our country. Instead it has been a beautiful garden, a paradise to gallop through, a path among the roads of life. It has been a good road for you, has it not?

CONSTANTINE: All my joy comes from my teacher, a good teacher.

MAXIMILIAN: Perhaps too good a teacher. And you have been too good a pupil because now they want to shoot you as well. In these modern times, that's the price of a good education. *(He laughs to himself and shivers slightly.)*

CONSTANTINE: It's inhuman. *(Constantine speaks to the room)*
Four days in here. Cold, damp. Musty. And I come to free you and

you won't even listen to me. Now, that is either a sign of madness or...

MAXIMILIAN: Or cowardice. So you think me a coward, eh?
(He laughs louder)

CONSTANTINE: Is the thought so amusing?

MAXIMILIAN: *(Listening intently)* Sh-h-h-h... Footsteps...Do you hear them?
(He pushes himself against the cellar wall.)
Yes, do you hear them?

CONSTANTINE: There's nothing. I hear nothing.

MAXIMILIAN: *(Recovering)* The water dripping. Yes. Just the water dripping. It seeps from the walls here…
(He rushes to one nearby wall.)
and splashes on the stone floor. *(He bends to the floor.)* It sounds like...drums. Constantine, is it cold in here?

CONSTANTINE: Please lie down here. Please. Listen to me this once.

MAXIMILIAN: Do you agree with me that it's cold?

CONSTANTINE: Yes, it's cold...much too cold.

MAXIMILIAN: Then I'll rest.
(Constantine helps Maximilian into his cot and then covers him.)
This window is so small it won't allow a star to shine her light inside my prison...There's a castle in Belgium like this place. Carlotta's parents' home, do you know it?

CONSTANTINE: Yes. It's a fine castle. Always in a constant state of holiday.

MAXIMILIAN: The people believe that it is comfortable because they could not live in it otherwise. Actually, its stones are only bigger. Its windows covered with expensive glass and because tapestries hang from the walls like carcasses in a butcher shop, everyone calls it beautiful. Carlotta and I would sit in the garden, by the shore, and stare at the sea. How she loved the sea. How she yearned to come here.

CONSTANTINE: Carlotta now yearns for you, Maximilian. She hasn't forgotten you but has become discouraged by the disposition of many of our European friends. You must be strong. You must return to her...
(Maximilian begins to fall asleep)

...all we need do now is signal the French. Then I will kill your guard and...

MAXIMILIAN: *(awakening)*
Rolpo? Oh, he won't like that, Constantine. He won't like that at all.

CONSTANTINE: He's an enemy and it must be done.

MAXIMILIAN: *(Sitting)* He'll be very disappointed especially since I've promised him wine...And the rest of the plan?

CONSTANTINE: The French will blow up this house while we escape to the horses outside.

MAXIMILIAN: And everyone inside.

CONSTANTINE: They are the enemy.

MAXIMILIAN: Ah. A very good plan. No doubt it is a French plan. Decidedly it is a French plan...And if Juarez should be killed in this explosion, who would lead Mexico?

CONSTANTINE: You, of course. Now I must signal the men.

MAXIMILIAN: There will be no signal, no killing; no explosion...I think my beard needs a trimming...Where are those scissors...

(Maximilian looks for the scissors and when he finds them, he begins to trim his beard.)

CONSTANTINE: Never. Never, could I believe that you who I have loved and admired could freeze so with fear that you are afraid to escape.

MAXIMILIAN: Maybe I am a coward. Yes, maybe that is the reason for my strange dreams, my action, my ambition. But if I am only a coward and a foolish fop who writes a book of etiquette as a legacy to his courage, then I have been one far too long to begin changing now...Now, get ready to leave. Or must I act like a stern father and give your rear a slapping?

CONSTANTINE: I cannot leave without you.

MAXIMILIAN: I am like my diary, a sea of memories. Once I was an Emperor. Now I am a prisoner... *(Listening)* Who hears drums, drums, the sound of drums. For four days. You know I can smell the drums—the felt from their thick blunt sticks which pound the stretched animal skins like heavy rain.

CONSTANTINE: Maximilian, you are ill. If you do not consent to leaving with me, then I must take you by force.
(There is noise outside as Juarez and Lopez ask where the guard is.)

VOICES: Now where is that Rolpo? He had strict orders to guard that Monarchist dog. Maybe he has escaped.

MAXIMILIAN: Constantine, for fear of your life. Quick. Hide.
(Constantine hides as Juarez and Lopez enter the cellar. Juarez is a bespectacled gentleman in the later part of his middle age. His face is drawn and he wears a long black coat. He has bushy eyebrows and he is of Mexican-Indian parentage. Lopez is of Spanish descent. He is a general and has a large mustache, shiny brass buttons, and an overbearing character.)

JUAREZ: At your liberty, we wish to speak with you over some very important matters.

MAXIMILIAN: Diplomacy and protocol, at war and peace. Yes, I will talk with you but, under these circumstances, please do not insinuate that I am receiving you at my liberty.

LOPEZ: Enough of this idle chitchat.
(Turning to Juarez)
Are we going to shoot the dog or aren't we?

MAXIMILIAN: A man of few words, your Lopez. I see his lust for my blood in his eyes.
(Facing Lopez)
How does victory taste? It burns the tongue with longing, does it not? Perhaps during your next battle, General, you will afford your adversary the courtesy of the daylight hours and possibly your next attack will be launched without the aid of traitors.

LOPEZ: The filthy, monarchist dog speaks of traitors. In this country, the only traitors are the pigs that support you. And not one of them will escape the sting of the Revolution.

JUAREZ: Please, Lopez. We have something to do.

LOPEZ: We should have shot him when we caught him.

MAXIMILIAN: Your one act of nobility. But then a dead Emperor in his nightclothes wouldn't have made a very heroic banner for the Revolution.

LOPEZ: *(So angry he can hardly speak.)* You aristocrat.

MAXIMILIAN: Juarez, do you have the same aversion to aristocrats? Do you think us all dogs?

JUAREZ: I have no aversion to aristocrats as persons, only as a symbol of an institution.

MAXIMILIAN: Instead, you want a democratic equality. Like Lopez, here. He's a man who wants equality because he fears anyone better than himself. His justice is that of an ignorant man trying to decide the fate of the intelligent. Justice with vengeance. Blood for the Revolution.

JUAREZ: Lopez has a zeal for methodology but not tact. Forgive him, but let us now discuss important matters...Wait here, Lopez. *(Juarez walks with Maximilian to the other side of the room.)* Lopez is quite militant in his desire to see you executed. He thinks it would be best for the Revolution.

MAXIMILIAN: Don't bother me with details.

JUAREZ: He's a good general but a shoddy humanitarian. Unfortunately, he is not alone in his position. I'm unlike him. Even though you are a foreign agent...

MAXIMILIAN: I am the agent of no one save my own ambition. As the Emperor of Mexico, I stand for the Mexican people.

JUAREZ: Well, then technically Maximilian—you can see my position—you are still a young man. And you have many friends. None to send you troops, thank God. But enough to cause the Revolution quite a bit of embarrassment if we execute you. I am an Indian but not a barbarian. Every hour more letters arrive pleading with me to spare your life. And life is precious.

MAXIMILIAN: The Old Government is part of my life. It lives inside me like a child.

JUAREZ: Exactly. And it has its supporters. The people, I tell you this frankly, seem to admire you in spite of your foreign ancestry. Listen, Maximilian, I'm even one of your admirers.

MAXIMILIAN: Eh. *(He laughs)* So we are not so different.

JUAREZ: How I wish I might have seen the expression of the landowners when you taxed their land, or those pompous Churchmen when you reformed their institution of religious slavery.

LOPEZ: *(Shouting to Juarez)*
Juarez, don't forget that this is the man who murders in the name of Monarchy, pillages for France, and robs for his own Empire.

MAXIMILIAN: If you don't mind my frankness, I think you have more to fear from him than me.

JUAREZ: To the troops, you are a symbol. Your death would give finality to our struggle and the people could return to plow their fields. But there is a way out.

MAXIMILIAN: Come, Juarez. We both know that there is no way. In fact, I'm already writing a chapter in my book on Executions. Stance. One should always walk briskly into place without dragging one's back.

JUAREZ: After the Revolution, you will be remembered for what you have given to Mexico—the hospitals, the universities, and a part of her culture. But now, while you talk of ruling—a man with no army—Mexico is gritting her teeth and remembering everything the Emperor did not give her.

MAXIMILIAN: She will not become great if she is spiteful.

JUAREZ: She will not become great if she is not united. Her development shall stop if her chosen leader is unable to patch her torn fabric together. I am asking for your help, Maximilian. Mexico will never be great if she remains divided. She will never be great if she remains poor. Forget your Empire. It is now a thing of history. The Empire is dead.

MAXIMILIAN: As long as I live, the Empire lives. And when I die, I'll take at least six feet of Empire with me. I am the Empire. The Empire is Maximilian. What do you want me to do, Juarez?

JUAREZ: I want you to abdicate your throne, denounce your opposition to the Revolution, and confess that you are a foreign agent sent to Mexico to exploit her for the French.

MAXIMILIAN: Do you actually believe that I will do that?

And then desert my Mexico?

JUAREZ: I thought you would leave if the need were great enough.

MAXIMILIAN: Never.

JUAREZ: Would you leave if I told you it would be for the sake of Mexico?

MAXIMILIAN: And run to Austria? The Empire with the tail between her legs? Did you know that when Louis Napoleon picked me to come to Mexico, I was the last person on his list? All the others refused. But not Maximilian. They called me foolish and young. Who would take a beautiful wife to a land of savages and mosquitoes? And we created a new life: for ourselves and for Mexico. Can I denounce a legacy? Can I abdicate my spirit? I would betray Mexico, myself, and the Empire more by leaving than by staying.

JUAREZ: But you could be free.

MAXIMILIAN: I am already free. But are you? Are you not a slave to your Revolution, to the whims of the Lopezes, and will you not be shackled by the will of that collection of ignorant opportunists, the Majority?

JUAREZ: Then I have no other choice. Under my hand, an act will be committed that I personally abhor. If I were only a man, I would flee. As the President, I must stay.

MAXIMILIAN: The Emperor of Mexico can do nothing less than that which the President would surely do. I answer only to myself and you must answer to others.

JUAREZ: Then in the name of the Revolution, we must commit this atrocity and I only hope it is the last.
(Juarez shakes Maximilian's hand)
The President of Mexico considers it an honor to have met the Emperor of Mexico. Long live Mexico.

MAXIMILIAN: Long live Mexico.

JUAREZ: Lopez, are you doing your best to confuse the situation or to help it? I wanted you to explain the relation of Maximilian to the Revolution but instead you stand here spouting unnecessary retorts. You are excused.

LOPEZ: The Revolution calls for the blood of this Aristocrat. This man who murders in the name of the Monarchy, who pillages for France, and robs for his own Empire.

MAXIMILIAN: General Lopez, with his over-zealous political conscience, is becoming quite tedious.

JUAREZ: Lopez, you can go now. Let me resolve some points with Maximilian. There is no need to have an emotional debate with a captive. *(Lopez exits.)*

MAXIMILIAN: *(To Juarez)* It's a shame that so many wars are won with slogans. The Revolution, bah. My leadership, and ways, were challenged by you and yours. I have lost and the best of a complex situation has been made simple. Like the drunkenness of that boy there—
(he indicates Constantine, still hiding, who feigns drunkenness)
whose greatest thought should now be whether he could steal my fine white mare without anybody noticing it.

JUAREZ: *(stares quizzically at Constantine, but then chooses to ignore him)* The soldiers want you dead to give some sort of ritual finality to their struggle.

MAXIMILIAN: Just tell me the time so that I may write in this book exactly when Maximilian took his last breath. As I told you before: I am writing a chapter on how to be executed. Execution: Part A: Stance.

JUAREZ: Please, there is so little time.

MAXIMILIAN: The man who is being executed must walk briskly into place. He should walk at a pace just slightly faster than the soldiers accompanying. He should never drag his back, nor give the impression of exhaustion no matter how tired he is.
(Maximilian starts coughing.)

JUAREZ: You aren't well.

MAXIMILIAN: I am fine. It's just too hot with these blankets.
(He takes them off.) Yes, the man should keep his hands directly at both sides, his head looking at the sky.

JUAREZ: For a man whom I believe loves life, you seem quite ready to give your own very easily. I am in many ways like you. I am older, perhaps, a little more cautious, a little more timid. But I love my Mexico. I love her enough to know that more than one man can love her.

MAXIMILIAN: But only one man can rule her.

JUAREZ: And only under the proper system of government...I think you love her too. Is it true that you ride from village to village and eat with the people?

MAXIMILIAN: That boy, there. *(indicates Constantine)* Yes, he's a fine rider. He and I used to go from the villages of my people to the mountains of my people. My wife Carlotta often would come. But through my countryside...I am not an exploiter. I have built academies instead of castles and hospitals instead of brothels.

JUAREZ: Yes, all true. All the reason why you are liked. But under the wrong system. For the Monarchy not the people, for the Empire of Maximilian not the inhabitants of Mexico...Later, after the Revolution, Mexico will never forget what you have done for her, but now she is thinking only about what you haven't done for her.

MAXIMILIAN: Have I been cruel?

JUAREZ: That is not the issue.

MAXIMILIAN: If I have, it was a misunderstanding. Have I ever been rash?

JUAREZ: That is not the issue.

MAXIMILIAN: When was I rash only because I am impetuous?

JUAREZ: The issue is that you are a Monarch. You have been able to make your customs Mexican but Mexico has been unable to make your customs hers. They like Maximilian, some even love him, some have died for him, but they detest the Emperor. The idea of a man lorded over them...You've adopted this country as an outsider and under false pretenses.

MAXIMILIAN: Juarez, must we discuss the merits of past facts? I am a captive. If you were mine we'd be discussing other things.

JUAREZ: Quite, quite, the war is over and all questions of legitimacy have been decided on the battlefields. Now we only have to worry about Mexico, and where she shall go.

MAXIMILIAN: She shall go nowhere if she is not united. She shall stagnate in her development if she is forced to have her seams ripped apart by internal dissension. She needs a good leader to patch her torn fabrics. She will never be great if she remains divided. She shall never be great if she remains poor.

JUAREZ: Now the division has been settled. Your men have surrendered and there is only one Mexican Army: The army of the people.

MAXIMILIAN: My army was also of the people.

JUAREZ: And the French will not aid you. The Sovereign sent from Europe is left with nothing more than an Ambassador pleading for his life and a drunken stable boy. Your Empire is dead, but Mexico is not.

MAXIMILIAN: The Empire is dead.

JUAREZ: I have come to speak to you as one man who cares more about his country than he does about his life. We live in a time when the people are restlessly calling for a New Way. Mexico, like many other lands, has been long under the domination of the European powers. I am the first to admit to you that these peoples have not always been unjust. But their initial biggest fault was that they were ...

MAXIMILIAN: European. Is not a man something more than his birthplace?

JUAREZ: Yes, yes many men are, but not their customs, not the faÁade they carry with them. That faÁade, no matter how ornamental to the new culture, is still only ornamental: something that is put on from without and not within.

MAXIMILIAN: I understand. But do you understand why it is I love Mexico, why I feel she is my child and I am her father?

JUAREZ: Perhaps it's because it is the only child you have, or that creating something is in all our men; something that will go on. We Indians have a legend about spirits lingering in the ancient deeds of men. But as I said before, we are not so different. Only I am the victor and you the...

MAXIMILIAN: Vanquished. Now what is it you want me to do? Shall I write out a statement abdicating my throne, relinquishing my Empire, and admonish myself back to Europe?

JUAREZ: That is what you must do. And then, possibly, you won't have to be shot.

MAXIMILIAN: And why am I to do this?

JUAREZ Because I think you would leave Mexico if the need were great enough.

MAXIMILIAN: Never on my own accounts.

JUAREZ: What if for her? Would you leave for her own sake?

MAXIMILIAN: (*Pauses, goes to Constantine, who still has his head down and runs his fingers through his hair.*)
Ah, to flee from my Mexico, just take my tail and place it between my legs, scurry home to Austria and pick up the pieces of a fragmented life. You know that every Monarch who Louis asked to become Emperor refused. Everyone. Only Foolish Maximilian, Silly Maximilian, Young Maximilian, he and his beautiful Belgium wife wanted to go to the land of mosquitoes and savages to create a new land. If this boy here could talk

he could tell you of our struggle and could tell you that Mexico is more than an Empire to me. No, I could never leave her. I would betray her more by leaving than I could possibly harm her by staying.

JUAREZ: But if you stay, as Lopez would say, the Revolution would demand your sacrifice. He wants to kill you because he fears you. But I fear killing more. I do not want to start a government from a pool of blood. But the soldiers and the people have been shouting, "Kill the European dogs" for so long, they would feel cheated if we didn't when we finally had one.

MAXIMILIAN: To the victors go their due.

JUAREZ: It's a filthy business. I thought maybe we could find a way for you to leave and be assured of your never returning.

MAXIMILIAN: Tomorrow morning?

JUAREZ: What?

MAXIMILIAN: Lopez will lead the firing squad. He shall snicker as he places me against the bullet-pocked wall with a final respectful shove, his own face shall be stone to hide his inner joy as the rifles are raised to send lead tearing through the bodies of the living. Would you want to die under the hand of anyone close?

JUAREZ: But do you have to? I don't want you to.

MAXIMILIAN: I know, you want me to sign some papers, which have no importance to either of us really, and renounce my claims and sit here and diplomatically scramble every which way to clutch onto my breaths. But there are some breaths not worth taking. I cannot lie, I cannot denounce myself, I cannot forsake my child though I realize, fully, that she has forsaken me.

JUAREZ: Then you are forcing me to commit an act that I can only abhor. If I were only a man I would flee, but as a leader I must stay and remain strong. I am the President of Mexico.

MAXIMILIAN: And I as Emperor of Mexico can do nothing less than what the President would surely do. I only have myself to answer to for the consequences of my act. You also have the people and possibly, though you might not realize it yet, even General Lopez. No

Juarez, your decision is in fact easier than mine since you have less control over how you will make it.

JUAREZ: Then the Revolution in the name of Democracy will be forced to commit another atrocity, though, God only knows and I hope it will be our last...But please, if you can... *(going near the stable lad)*
Warn your squire...

MAXIMILIAN: Constantine.

JUAREZ: Maybe send your stable lad here to tell him that General Lopez is proceeding with a house-by-house search for him with the most religious fervor. For some reason his troops are as fascinated with the killing of a young Aristocrat as they are with killing you... *(Badly)* It is not easy to be a leader.

MAXIMILIAN: It is not easy.

JUAREZ: To see a man die that you preferred lived; so that he would raise his family.

MAXIMILIAN: My family is Mexico and my life is in this countryside. *(Softly)* Juarez, Mexico will be in safe hands. The

Emperor of Mexico has been greatly honored to meet his Excellency, the President of Mexico. Long live Mexico.

JUAREZ: *(Exiting and softly)* Long live Mexico.

CONSTANTINE: *(Jumping up as soon as Juarez leaves)*
Long live Maximilian.

MAXIMILIAN: *(Sitting and shivering. Constantine helps him put on blankets he has taken off.)*
Where is Rolpo with that extra blanket? The damp crawls under your skin. Now, boy, get yourself ready to leave.

CONSTANTINE: That Juarez. He's a shrewd one. Acting as if he can be trusted.

MAXIMILIAN: He can be trusted. Now get ready.

CONSTANTINE: But we have to leave together, Maximilian. We must. We'll go to Europe and raise funds. Once you spoke to Napoleon, he'd listen. Thousands of troops. Good Austrian soldiers, the Swiss guards, Italian...

MAXIMILIAN: We'd bring war.

CONSTANTINE: We'd restore Maximilian to his throne and cast away the pretender Juarez.

MAXIMILIAN: And what does he pretend? That he is an Emperor and that Mexico is his family that he can propagate by increasing some territorial domain?

CONSTANTINE: Juarez must be stopped.

MAXIMILIAN: Why, he's a man who believes in what he says. Sometimes, though not often, he will be the victim of his own sincerity, but never his passion. Such a man is a good ruler. I think my beard needs another trimming. *(Looking for a small package)*
Ah, here it is. No glass, but I'll manage.
(He takes out a small scissors and begins to trim his beard.) Yes, one must look his best no matter what the conditions.

CONSTANTINE: Maximilian, we must go. Are you getting ready to leave?

MAXIMILIAN: I cannot leave with you, my dear friend. My life has passed inside a dream...and the sound of drums.

CONSTANTINE: I don't hear any drums.

MAXIMILIAN: We cannot let Mexico have her frail body scarred by more wars.

CONSTANTINE: We could liberate her.

MAXIMILIAN: And in the ensuing cascades of blood we would destroy what I love most. It is better to let some dreams die in their sleep.

CONSTANTINE: *(Putting on his coat and preparing to leave.)*
And I'll go to my parents and to Carlotta and to all of Europe and tell them that I rode with a great horseman who once faltered and I left behind.

MAXIMILIAN: That you turned behind, and found you couldn't help because the man's body was sound but his soul was damaged and you had to leave before you suffered injury to yourself...before you began to hear the drums in the middle of your nights.

CONSTANTINE: *(Starting to cry)*
I'll signal to the men.

MAXIMILIAN: Nonsense, you'll do as you're told.

CONSTANTINE: Then I'll break open the door myself. *(He tugs at the door. Tugging harder)* I'm not going to let them kill you.

MAXIMILIAN: *(Going to the door.)* All you have to do is turn the handle.

CONSTANTINE: Why, it's open.

MAXIMILIAN: It always has been.

ROLPO: *(Voice off stage.)* I've found it. I've found you a blanket.

MAXIMILIAN: *(Putting Constantine back into his drunken position.)* Now play the drunk again. I'll get Rolpo to take you out. *(Rolpo enters)*

ROLPO: Good colors. You like the colors.

MAXIMILIAN: Not especially, but let's see if it's warm. Yes it is. Fine. Now you can take my stable lad out of here.

ROLPO: What's his problem? Don't look too good to me, I suppose.

MAXIMILIAN: He's been drinking.

ROLPO: Let me at it. You promised me some wine. And now I could use it for General Lopez yelled at me for bringing you a stranger and getting you a blanket. That's sure a mean General.

MAXIMILIAN: I'll give you all the wine you want after you take this lad away. He needs a strong man like you to carry him.

ROLPO: How do I know there'll be any wine left if I go? They may come and shoot you and close up this cellar. No, I'm not moving till I get me drink.

MAXIMILIAN: But just a little.

ROLPO: Sure. *(Max gives him a bottle of wine. Rolpo starts swallowing it hungrily.)* Good, good grapes. Can't get much of this around here, only purple water, that's what it is. Things was a little better in your Army.

MAXIMILIAN: You were in my Army?

ROLPO: Sure I was. Lots of us were, till we got the call to Demo, democracy. Yea, Revolution.

MAXIMILIAN: Wasn't my army a happy army?

ROLPO: Sure was, a good one, a might too clean if you ask me, having us wash all the time. Here you can be a little more casual. I'm a casual man, you know.

MAXIMILIAN: No I didn't. Are you done?

ROLPO: On one bottle. Give me another.

MAXIMILIAN: *(To the boy.)* Can you stand?

CONSTANTINE: Yes, sir.

ROLPO: Don't even look like he drunk, he's a strange one.

MAXIMILIAN: Here, here's another bottle. Now will you lead this poor boy out of here to the street? Please.

ROLPO: Now look, your Kingship, we made a deal and I ain't going to try and get out of it. No, I got you the blanket and now I have to take my punishment. That's what this is, it's punishment for leaving my post. Oh, Juarez, he don't care, got me guarding a man in a cellar that has no lock.

CONSTANTINE: *(To Rolpo.)* What did you say?

ROLPO: Say, who is this?

CONSTANTINE: What'd you say about the door? Isn't it closed?

ROLPO: Now, let me look. No, the door is opened. Isn't that right, your Kingship?

MAXIMILIAN: Yes.

ROLPO: But it was closed. I can remember distinctly that it was closed. Only it got no lock, so I don't understand who cares whether it's open or closed. More wine.

MAXIMILIAN: That's enough. You've got to take this lad away.

CONSTANTINE: And what makes you so sure I want to go?

ROLPO: *(To Maximilian, very drunk.)* Yea, what makes you so sure?

MAXIMILIAN: Because you've got reason to live and a future to prepare.

ROLPO: *(Finding a new bottle by himself.)* Yup, I'll drink to that. Say it again.

MAXIMILIAN: Now my fine blossom of the People's Democratic Armies, will you stand up like a fighting man and take my lad....

ROLPO: Who said, fighting man. Who said it?

MAXIMILIAN: I did.

ROLPO: Oh, thought it was you. Well there's some that fights.

MAXIMILIAN: Yes, now will you stand up and take the boy?

ROLPO: *(Stands up and gestures like a fighter)*
And some that don't fight.
(He falls down doing a boxing stance.)
And some that don't fight.
(on the floor) I don't fight.

CONSTANTINE: But if the door is open we can both escape, easily.

MAXIMILIAN: I can't, can't you understand that I can't leave my country?

CONSTANTINE: Do you think it is any easier to leave a friend?

ROLPO: *(Singing.)* I drink today before the lights go out, I drink today before the lights go out and nobody serves any more wine. Drink, drink, drink, drink, down your muzzled, as you guzzle all the night till light.

MAXIMILIAN: Now, we've got to get Rolpo up so he can take you out. He couldn't recognize the rear of a horse from a stable lad, but if Lopez comes… *(Maximilian tries to pick up Rolpo who gleefully falls down.)*

CONSTANTINE: Then I would be recognized and join you in the morning to take our last ride in the sun.

ROLPO: I'll drink to that. Drink, drink, drink, down the muzzle, guzzle, guzzle.

CONSTANTINE: You can leave here, we can return.

MAXIMILIAN: Upon the heels of destruction. No, there has to be some finality for this Revolution as there has to be for the human life. Life is inscribed between two points. And as Mexico once called for my life to help her, it now calls for my death for much the same reasons.

CONSTANTINE: And I can't leave you to go out and be alone.

MAXIMILIAN: Rolpo, get up this instant and take this boy out of here.

ROLPO: I'll drink to that.

CONSTANTINE: *(As Maximilian tries to lift Rolpo)* I'm not leaving you.

LOPEZ: *(Voice off-stage)* Rolpo.

ROLPO: I'll drink to that.

CONSTANTINE: I'm staying with my Emperor. I'm too scared to do anything else.

MAXIMILIAN: Dear Rolpo, probably one of the finest men in his People's Democracy's Army, a demon. Ha, ha. *(Laughs then coughs)* Sh-h-h, it's the sound of drums.

CONSTANTINE: The sound of drums? Give me your hand.

MAXIMILIAN: The soil of Mexico will remember us.

ROLPO: *(Drunk and on the floor)* I'll drink to that.

LOPEZ: *(Entering)* What's this? *(Pause)* More blood for the Revolution.

MAXIMILIAN: No, it's only the sound of heartbeats of men too brave or too scared to live.

(The sound of muffled drums is heard. The film, from the beginning of the play, is projected onto the backstage wall. This time the figures are clearer and Maximilian and Constantine can be made out to be marching to their deaths, with Lopez leading the executioners. The executioners take aim as the drums sound loudly and then the picture begins to fade out.)

THE END

Cry of the Boy

CRY OF THE BOY

Setting: *The stage is divided into two rooms, a large modern living room and a smaller bedroom. The living room is in American Modern and has a Book-of-the-Month Club veneer. The upstage wall has a large dust-free rectangular shape on it. It looks like an old painting has been recently removed. There is a card table in the room, a bookcase and a kitchen bar. A red balloon hangs from the ceiling in the living room.*

Characters:

Kid

Is a 17-year-old with smooth skin and straight hair. He dresses in plain, youngish clothes. He is very "cute." He is very intelligent but has been conditioned to act as if he were only 13.

Momma

Is an attractive woman in her mid-30's. She is a very sexy dresser. She combines a Park Avenue intellect with a Bronx background.

Papa
Is a neater and younger Man in the Grey Flannel Suit*. *He is easy-going and is used to not getting angry.*

(Curtain Up. The Kid enters the living room from his bedroom. As soon as he enters the living room, he begins to look for "something." As he looks, he whistles part of Trois Morceaux en Form de Poire, *by Erick Satie. As the Kid is looking, a light comes up and shows Papa sitting at the step of one of the wings, reading the newspaper. The Kid stops looking and arranges the living room furniture in a slalom pattern. Momma now enters the theatre and is guided to her seat by a matron, a follow spot is used. Momma is seated by the wing opposite from Papa. As she sits, the Kid takes his scooter and dashes between the furniture.)*

Momma: *(From her seat near the wing.)* Hey Kid, Kid.
(The Kid continues to dash between the furniture.)
Hey Kid. *(Momma runs up to the stage. She shouts)*
Hey Kid. Hey Kid.
(The Kid continues to dash between the furniture.)

Hey Kid, Hey Kid.

Kid: *(Comes to an abrupt stop.)* Yes Momma, did you say something?

*Editor's note: A novel, by Sloan Wilson, about a New York corporate executive. The 1956 movie version starred Gregory Peck and Jennifer Jones.

Momma: Yes I did Kid. *(Kid hugs his scooter.)* How many times did I tell you to never run the Winter Olympics in here?

Kid: Every time that I do it, Momma. *(He goes to put his scooter away, upstage in the living room.)*

Momma: That's right.

Kid: *(Proudly)* Thank you, Momma.

Momma: You're welcome, Kid. *(She pats Kid on the head.)* You always tell the truth to your Momma. How come you always tell the truth, Kid? How come you never lie like all the other kids do?

Kid: *(Goes to hug his scooter.)* Yes I do. I do all the time.

Momma: There you go, doing it again. You did it again, you know. Can't you stop doing it?

Kid: No.

Momma: Did it again. *(Kid hides behind a piece of furniture. Momma turns around to look for him and he rushes to her and hugs her.)*

Kid: I love you.

Momma: Would you like to play a game?

Kid: Yes, so very much. What shall we play?

Momma: How about….*(She draws it out.)*

Kid: *(Excited)* Yes, yes.

Momma: How about…. *(Draws it out again.)*

Kid: Yes, yes. About what?

Momma: Bridges. How about playing bridges?

Kid: Which bridge, which bridge?

Momma: The London Bridge.

Kid: That bridge is too foggy and I haven't a raincoat.

(Momma goes to the card table.)

Momma: Have you a handkerchief?

Kid: Yes.

Momma: With you?

Kid: *(Takes out his handkerchief and then he puts it away.)*
Weren't you the London Bridge last time?

Momma: And the time before that.

Kid: And the time before that.

Momma: And the time before the time before that.

Kid: Will you be the London Bridge?

Momma: Of course. Are you ready?
(Kid goes to get his scooter.)

Kid: Almost. *(He starts to warm up.)* Ready.

Momma: *(Raises up the table.)* Bridge up.
(Kid gets ready to dash under, but Momma quickly slams the table down.)

Bridge down.

Kid: *(Stops for a second, then he rushes over to Momma and hugs her.)* I love you.

Momma: I love you too.

Kid: And I love you too.

Momma: Now clean up, little darling. Harry and Emma are coming.

Kid: Are Harry and Emma really coming?

Momma: Yes.

Kid: *(Starts cleaning up and putting the furniture back.)*
Who's Harry and Emma?

Momma: *(Dusts the furniture)*

They're your brother and sister, Kid.

Kid: What are their names?

Momma: Call them Mr. Harry and Emma.

Momma: *(Starts to fix her dress)*

Hey Kid, can you get the mirror?

(Kid exits and comes back on stage with a huge mirror.)

Hold it up. Want your Momma to look good? Hey Kid, how do I look?

Kid: *(Speaks from behind the mirror.)* More beautiful than….

Momma: *(Not really paying attention.)* Than what….

Kid: Than the first day I saw you.

Momma: I think that's them, Kid. Hurry, and put it away.

(Kid puts the mirror away and Momma rushes from furniture piece to piece, making sure everything is in order. At this time Papa, in a follow spot, puts down his paper and puts a sign on the wing. The sign reads: THE AMERICAN ARMY MARCHES INTO MOSCOW.)

Momma: Papa.

Papa: Momma.

Momma: Hello Papa.

Papa: Hello Momma.

Momma: What are you doing?

Papa: Just business, and it's none of yours.

Momma: You're mediocre.

Papa: No, I'm a sign carrier.

Momma: There is no difference.

Papa: How's the Kid?

Momma: What do you care?

Papa: What, what, didn't I go through thick and thin, hot and cold, positive and negative, for her?

Momma: For him, you always forget.

Papa: What of it? Are you holding it against me?

Momma: Yes, at the least.

Papa: Is *he* going to make *his* move?

Momma: Yes. He has to, doesn't he?

Papa: Of course.

Momma: Of course.

Momma: Good-bye, Papa.

Papa: *(Papa goes back to reading his paper.)*

Good-bye, Momma.

Momma: Hey Kid, come on out.

Kid: *(Comes back onto the stage.)* Here I am.

Momma: I know. *(She straightens out his clothes, to the smallest detail.)* There. Now don't forget to say to them what I told you.

Kid: What?

Momma: Did you forget what I told you?

Kid: No, no.

Momma: Are you sure?

Kid: Positive.

Momma: Positive?

Kid: Shoot you for it.

Momma: You wouldn't.

Kid: I would so. No backs, no penny tax, or no backs.

Momma: *(Both Momma and Kid wind up their hands for odds and evens.)* Once.

Kid: Twice.

Momma & Kid: Shoot. *(Neither moves.)*

Kid: I win, I win.

Momma: Well....

Kid: I did, I did.

Momma: Yes, but be good.

(Momma now directs herself to an imaginary door in center stage.) Coming, coming.

Momma: *(Momma goes to open the door and the Kid begins looking for something again. Momma speaks to Harry and Emma; Harry and Emma are invisible.)*
Well hello Harry, . . . hello Emma. It's been a long time. Come in. No, I'm not busy at all. I was just going to beat the Kid. Want to watch?

(She closes the door and directs Harry and Emma to some chairs.)

Well, let me look at you. You're simply beautiful Harry…You look good too, Emma. Married life does you well. Hey Kid. Come on over and say something.

Kid: What should I say?

Momma: Just come over. You can think of something later.

Momma: He's just a little bit shy. As a matter of fact, he just hasn't any guts.

Kid: Momma.

Momma: Kid.

Kid: I love you.

Momma: Then shall we dance?

Kid: Dance.

Momma: Yes. Remember how?

Kid: Not too well. The dancing teacher told me....

Momma: What did she tell you?

Kid: *(A little ashamed)* She told me that I should just sort of stand still and clap.

Momma: Wonderful. Then I'll dance and you stand in place and clap your hands. Harry and Emma will like it.

Kid: They will?

Momma: Of course. I've told them about all the things we do together. After all, what are families for. Watch us now Harry and Emma—this is a dancing family.
(She starts to dance.)

Kid, we need some music.

(Kid stands-in-place and begins to clap his hands.)

Momma: Kid, we need some music. (*Kid doesn't listen. Momma shouts.)* Kid. Kid. (*Kid's clapping becomes more frenzied.)* Kid. *(Momma now whispers.)*
Hey, Kid.

Kid: Yes Momma.

Momma: A record. *(Kid goes to put on a record.)* Back in the Bronx, we didn't dance too much. Did I ever tell you kids about the parties we had with the people from the old country? With the wine flowing in a thousand foreign languages. And Grandma and Grandpa, giggling after a few. Those were parties. Uncle Simon, the life of the party—always ripping his clothes off.

Kid: The record is ready.

(Kid puts on the record. It's "That's Me Zorba," from the album Zorba The Greek. *Momma begins to dance. The Kid stands in place and claps his hands. Momma gets a veil and swings it around, tempting Harry. Momma speaks while she dances.)*

Momma: Dancing lessons are so important, nowadays. I keep telling the Kid that. It's the way you meet people, get to know them. How else, if you don't play golf? The prices of lessons vary. You have to pay for what you get. From Ginger Rogers to pitter-patter. Kid's not too bad. Sure do look good, Harry. Sure are big, Harry. I wonder if you're as big....

(She begins panting and rubs the veil across her chest as if it were a towel.)

Dancing is music. Music is dancing. Better than
(Stretches out the words)

Ovaltine or artichoke hearts….

(She swoons and the Kid catches her. Kid put her down and then shuts off the record player. He then begins to look for something and whistles the Satie song.)

Momma: *(Begins to awaken. She is a little intoxicated.)*
That Kid's some dancer. Hope I didn't miss his move.

(She looks at him; he is still looking for something.) No not yet. Hey Kid, Harry and Emma are here.

Kid: *(Stops looking and comes over to Momma and hugs her.)*

Hello Harry and Emma.

Momma: Is that anyway to speak to your brother and sister?

Kid: Hello Mr. Harry and Emma.

Momma: Hey Harry and Emma, did I ever tell you about the Kid's sense of humor? Wait, Kid, show Harry and Emma your sense of humor.

Kid: Clean or dirty?

Momma: Which do you think?

Kid: There once was a man who wanted more than anything else to teach his donkey to live without ... He told his friend this one day.

Momma: Please try not to screw it up dear. Without what?

Kid: Didn't I say it?

Momma: No.

Kid: Maybe you didn't hear it?

Momma: Maybe.

Kid: Well this time I'll either say it or you'll hear it.

Momma: Good.

Kid: This man tells his friend that he wants to teach his donkey how to live without food. Well, the friend does not see his friend, the one with the donkey, for almost three weeks. And when the friend sees his friend, he asks him: "How did your thing go with your donkey?" And the other friend replies: "Not too good, my friend. I have suffered a grievous loss. When my donkey had finally learned how to go without food …"

Momma: You're screwing it up again dear. When he finally taught his donkey how to go without food, what happened?

Kid: It died.

Momma: Well anyway, he plays the guitar. Really. He practices all the time. He never goes out anymore. Never plays with all his little friends. Hey Kid, don't you have any more little friends to play with?

Kid: I play the guitar.

Momma: Will you play for Harry and Emma?

Kid: *(Goes and gets his guitar.)* Yes. I like playing the guitar.

Momma: *(Kid picks up the guitar and starts to play. He is very good.)*
Well play then.

(Kid stops.)

Often, when we are not dancing, the Kid will fill the house with the music of his guitar. At least that's what he tells me—I'm usually not at home when he plays. Nothing against the instrument, mind you; I just hate noise. I get nosebleeds. Really, it's very embarrassing, not to mention messy. *(Kid puts down the guitar and begins to look for something and whistle his Satie song.)*

Momma: He's certainly getting old. Why, I could just eat him up. And you know *(she whispers)* he is getting hair. Do you want him to show it all, to you? Hey Kid.

Kid: *(Stops looking and races over to Momma.)*
Is it time for another bath?

Momma: No, we just took one a few hours ago.

Kid: And before that, a few hours before that.

Momma: And before that, a few hours before that.

Kid: Can we take one a few hours after that? Can we? Can we?

Momma: And a few hours after that.

Kid: I love you. Is it time for the beating?

Momma: Did you think I forgot?

Kid: No.

Momma: Then are you ready? *(She goes to one side of the room.)*

Kid: Yes, I'm ready. *(He goes to the other side of the room.)*

Momma: Remember Harry and Emma are here.

Kid: I won't forget.

Momma: Begin. *(They both take a step in and stamp their feet.)*

Momma & Kid: Ten, eight, five, three, two, one

(They both scream)

Now. *(Neither moves.)*

Momma: How do you feel?

Kid: Tired. Can I go rest?

Momma: Certainly. But say goodnight.

Kid: *(Kid leaves and calls back.)* Goodnight Mr. Harry and Emma.

(Kid enters his room and puts on a light. Momma gets a deck of cards and begins to deal.)

Momma: Now we can play some Bridge. *(Kid closes the door and the living room is blackened.)*

(Kid whistles his song and looks for something. Then he sits on the bed in his room. He turns on his tape recorder.)

Tape: Hello. *(Tape is of Kid's voice)*

Kid: Hello.

Tape: How are you today?

Kid: I'm fine, thank you.

Tape: You're welcome. Do you want to play?

Kid: Yes. What shall we play?

Tape: Let's play MonopolyÆ. I like that.

Kid: I like that too but I don't know how to play.

Tape: Neither do I. Let's play something else.

Kid: Yes. What shall we play?

Tape: Let's play Questions?

Kid: We played that yesterday.

Tape: And the yesterday before yesterday.

Kid: And the yesterday before that yesterday.

Tape: Yes. Do you want to play?

Kid: Yes. I want to play.

Tape: First Question: When? *(Kid doesn't answer.)*

Wrong. Second Question: How? *(Kid looks around.)*
No, wrong. This is a double Question, they're a little harder. Ready?

Kid: Ready.

Tape: Why and What? *(Kid fidgets a bid.)* Time's up, wrong. Final question: Who?

Kid: Who?

Tape: Don't stall. Wrong, wrong, wrong. Five out of five, including a double.

Kid: I almost knew the last one.

Tape: That's not good enough. Did you find it?

Kid: No.

Tape: Giving up?

Kid: No, just looking.

Tape: It's all the same unless you find it.

Kid: I know.

Tape: Are you sure?

Kid: Almost sure.

Tape: That's not good enough.

Kid: Will it be good, if I find it?

Tape: Very good.

Kid: How good?

Tape: As good as gumdrops.

Kid: I don't like gumdrops.

Tape: Neither do I.

Kid: Then it will be good.

Tape: Yes, as good as gumdrops.

Kid: But I haven't found it.

Tape: You've been looking.

Kid: But not finding.

Tape: Then do something.

Kid: What?

Tape: What is left?

Kid: I don't know. I don't know.

Tape: Good. Good. This is the first step.

Kid: I don't think that I'll ever find it.

Tape: Wonderful. But are you resigned?

Kid: No, I still want to find it.

Tape: Bad.

Kid: How bad?

Tape: As bad as gumdrops.

Kid: Then I'll become resigned.

Tape: Commit yourself to it.

Kid: I don't understand. I have been looking and haven't found.

Tape: Then find and do not look.

Kid: Is that the answer, is that the answer?

Tape: No, that is not the answer.

Kid: What is the answer?

Tape: The answer is Bandersnatch.

Kid: Bandersnatch?

Tape: Yes, Bandersnatch.

Kid: Bandersnatch.

Tape: Shall I play something for you?

Kid: Yes.

(The music comes on and it is the Kid's Satie song. The Kid then opens his door a very little bit. He hears his mother speak.)

Momma: Emma, why don't you go to the bathroom; we'll finish the game when you come back. Now Harry, please keep your filthy hands off the top of my dress. Don't start becoming rational. I've heard them all before. Don't you realize that Emma is sitting right next to you. Neighbors talk you know.

(Sensuously)

Under what? Harry, what shall we do with Emma? And look who, hello Emma. Harry and I were just talking about you. Why don't you have any clothes on, dear? Harry, that's no way for your wife to walk around. That idea is disgusting, Harry. Who'd you say gets on the bottom. Oh, we all just roll around, huh. Harry, you needn't be so frantic.

(The Kid has been putting together the piece of a cardboard house, on his floor. Papa puts down his paper and with follow spot puts a new sign up. It reads: THE SPECIAL FORCES RAPE THE MOSCOW BALLET—A 2nd COMING. He returns to his paper.)

Momma: Now he's gone too far. Filthy-minded sign carrier.
(Papa comes back and pastes a strip of paper over the sign; it reads: CENSORED.)

Papa: I was just minding my business. *(Momma speaks from blackened stage.)*

Momma: Business is getting awfully vulgar these days.

Papa: Lucky, I don't live home. 'Cause of my allergy.

Momma: Not that again. Couldn't you just get hay fever like other people?

Papa: Difference is a quality to cherish.

Momma: Do you still love those what-do-you callits?
(Kid begins to light matches and watch them burn.)

Papa: You mean H-bombs?

Momma: Yes.

Papa: I love them.

Momma: That isn't normal, Papa.

Papa: Yes, I'm Papa; but as Momma always says:

(Momma speaks and Papa mouths the words)
"Don't be fooled by titles."

(Papa goes back to his papers.)

Momma: Something's wrong in the Kid's room. Look, a Momma can smell these things. *(She rushes into the Kid's room.)* How many times have I told you never to do that?

Kid: Every time that I do it.

Momma: Still telling the truth?

Kid: Sometimes.

Momma: There you go doing it again. I'll put them out.
(Momma exits and the Kid quickly wraps up his house in a blanket, puts the blanket in a suitcase and throws the suitcase under his bed. Momma runs in with some water. She puts the water down where she sees that there is no longer a fire.)

Momma: Did it again.

Kid: Yes, again like before.

Momma: Maybe next time you won't.

Kid: Maybe next time you won't.

Mom: Maybe.

Kid: Maybe.

Momma: Come on out. I think Harry and Emma are going to be leaving soon.

(Kid shuts off his tape recorder and exits to the living room. When he shuts off the light, the living room's lights come up. Momma sits down at the card table. The Kid plays with his scooter on the floor.)

Did you ever see the Kid's artwork? This one *(she goes over to the wall where the removed painting is. She runs her hand over the painting's outline.)*

This is his largest work; my little Kid, the Picasso. Tell them what you call it.

Kid: I call it *Stolen.*

Momma: He's very imaginative. He's got a smaller one in his room. What do you call that one, Kid?

Kid: I call that one *Missing. (At this point the Kid walks directly under the red balloon, which is hanging from the ceiling, and he stands still.)*

Momma: Oh, must you go Harry, we were having so much fun, Tiger. I'm not busy, I was just going to beat the Kid. Want to watch? OK, another time then.
(She opens up the imaginary door and then closes it.)

Momma: Hey Kid, what's the matter? You're not looking anymore.

Kid: I will not look anymore. I have been looking day after day.

Momma: After day.

Kid: After day.

Momma: You've been looking a hell-of-a-lot, Kid.

Kid: Not any more.

Momma: Are you sure?

Kid: Yes, I'm sure.

Momma: How sure?

Kid: As sure as gumdrops?

Momma: Well then here it is. *(She points to the red balloon. Kid doesn't look.)*

Kid: Nothing is there.

Momma: Don't you want to find it?

Kid: No. (*Papa places a new sign, it reads: World War III– A Happening In One Whimper.)*

Momma: Papa, the Kid is going to make his move.

Papa: I knew it. Did he? *(The Kid falls into a crumple position.)*

Papa: Is that what you mean?

Momma: So he doesn't make big moves. Hey Kid, don't you want to make your move?

Papa: Kid, don't you want to be important?

(To Momma.) Did he find it?

Momma: He won't look.

Papa: Come on Kid. We'll show it to you.

Kid: *(Rises, he's still a little hunched over.)* No, I will not look.

Papa: But it's right here. *(He points to the balloon.)*

Kid: *(Straightens up some more.)* Nothing is there.

Momma: Kid, Kid here it is.

Kid: No, nothing is there. *(He is now standing, proudly erect)*

(Lights off.)

Momma: Make your move. *(She takes a step toward the Kid. When lights come up, Momma, Papa and Kid are all still but in different step by step positions . Lights down.)*

Papa: Make your move. *(He and Momma move toward the Kid, by a step and the Kid moves away from them. Lights up. This same pattern—speak and take a step in the dark and then lights up to a still stage— is continued.)*

Momma: Move. Make your move. Move.

Papa: Make it.

(Pace quickens.)

Momma: Make…

Papa: Your move.

Momma & Papa:Make-Your-Move.

Momma & Papa:Make-Your-Move.

Momma & Papa:Move.

Momma & Papa:Move.

Kid: *(As the Kid is cornered, he screams defiantly.)*

Bandersnatch. Bandersnatch. Bandersnatch.

(This is a complete blackout and then the lights come up only in the Kid's room. Kid goes to his tape recorder and puts it on.)

Tape: Hello.

Kid: Hello.

Tape: How are you today?

Kid: Today, today I am fine.

Tape: Shall I play for you?

Kid: Yes. *(He takes out the suitcase from under his bed. Unwraps the house that is inside the blanket and then takes out the house. He lights a match to the house and it goes up into flames. He watches the flames.)*

Tape: I love you.

Kid: I love you.

Tape: I love you too.

Kid: I love you too.

Tape: I love you too. I love you too. *(Voice slowly fades as the curtain comes down.)* I love you too. I love you too.

THE END

The Devil and Don Quijote

The Devil and Don Quijote

Scene:

An open field with a triangular road running through it. Downstage is clear except for some shrubs on either side; upstage center there are some rocks and upstage right there is a hill.

Characters

Don Quijote

Has just escaped from an old age home and is wearing a homemade suit of armor with a pot as a helmet. He is wearing nightclothes under his armor. He has a stiff, straight mustache and goatee. He has a long lance.

Sancho Panza

Was the Don's attendant and has helped him escape. He is wearing dirty whites, which are held up by a rope. He has a well-creased hat that he uses for gesticulation. He is very fat.

Banker

Is well-dressed and fastidious. He has on a tropical suit and a fine white hat and an expensive brimcloth. Call him Alejandro.

Lady
She is the Banker's wife and is always fashionably dressed. She has on high heels. Her hairstyle is flamboyant Spanish and she wears a diamond tiara.

Driver
Wears a modified chauffeur's uniform with black cap. His name is Juan.

Faterio
An old man who has been running wild in the mountains for years. He has a beard and a staff.

Diablo
He is young with a moustache, goatee, with a miniature lance.

Setting:

Spain in post-revolutionary times. It's about 3:00 P.M. at the open field and the guns still feel hot. (enter the Don who has just recently escaped the confines of an old age home).

DON QUIJOTE: Hey Sancho, we can rest now. We're well away. Tie up Rocinante, my trusty steed, upon whose back today I charged from the grips of the Enchanter; my noble stallion who shall carry me into the excitement of countless battles and the glories of numerous victories.

SANCHO: *(Sancho's voice off-right)*

I cannot tie her up my SeÒor because she has fallen down.

DON QUIJOTE: Leave her rest, God knows she has earned it. . . . Soon some benevolent king shall reward Rocinante with a golden saddle—which I shall proudly ride upon. Please bring me some lunch to fill the grumblings of a restless stomach.
(The Don looks over the field as he waits for Sancho.)

SANCHO: *(Enter Sancho carrying a workman's lunch pail)*
SeÒor, you know, I think if Rocinante gets a golden saddle it had better be soon or light. Her belly sags almost to the ground. But I respect her more for it. You shall ride her into glory and I shall walk with you there. But if you don't mind my opinion SeÒor….

DON QUIJOTE: Not now, Sancho. Now tell me what food we have. I am hungry, and how can the world's greatest knight errant battle the wicked to death and right all the humanity's wrongs on an empty stomach?
(The Don goes to the hill, stage right, and makes an effort to sit. He is balanced on his lance in a pose that is reminiscent of one-hand tree swinging.)

SANCHO: *(Opens his pail.)*
There is some cheese, which is a little green, some bread, which is a little soggy and a few apples. This food isn't fit for a knight. Besides there is only enough for one.

DON QUIJOTE: Yes Sancho. In times of stress even knights must make sacrifices, and I shall always remember the noble sacrifices that you have made for me. Together we shall create chivalric history and rewards, though few now, shall be many. Sit. Sit.
(With some effort Sancho manages to get the Don seated.)

SANCHO: (*Sits next to the Don and places the food on his hand and he savors each piece.)*
Yes, you are right, before I helped you escape from the confinement of the Evil Enchanter I didn't even know there was one. I was then only the simple attendant at Don Luis' Old Age Home but now I am a squire to a famous knight errant and soon I shall be rewarded with a kingdom of my own; no longer am I tricked by any enchantment.

DON QUIJOTE: *(The Don has found a handkerchief, from inside his armor, and now he places the food on his lap as Sancho looks on flabbergasted.*)

If you only will have some patience, valour, goodness. Sancho, you shall have your kingdom soon.

SANCHO: *(Sancho looks on flabbergasted.)*
Excuse me. *(Don pays no heed)*
Excuse me SeÒor, but what am I to eat, my hat?

DON QUIJOTE: You seem to do everything else possible to it.

SANCHO: *(Sancho gives a vivid demonstration of his hunger pains.)*
Oh Señor, even my hat couldn't fill my hunger. I am so hungry that my head aches like a bathtub full of dishes and my feet are swelled like the mountain's pebbles and my tongue *(he sticks it out)* is so tangled that I can hardly talk.

DON QUIJOTE: We must learn how to take the good with the bad or is it the bad with the good? Anyway, listen Sancho…I think that we shall have a great adventure today. I feel it in my bones.

SANCHO: With a little liniment and a rubdown . . .

DON QUIJOTE: Maybe later Sancho, I mean that today I feel like I have just been born. I'm sure that a suitable glorious experience shall come along to complement the occasion.

SANCHO: I hope it is more suitable than the beating I took on our first adventure at the inn.

DON QUIJOTE: That only appeared to be an inn, Sancho. It was really a dungeon and the tremendous gallantry we displayed in fighting our way out of it shall make a very notable beginning exploit in the career of Don Quijote and his squire Sancho. It won't be long that our names shall be famous and you will have that kingdom that I promised you…Let the pleasant thoughts of the future fill your stomach.

SANCHO: Thank you SeÒr, but I feel that if I don't eat today I will have no future. I can't wait until I own the kingdom you promise me, only so far I have felt only misery instead of comfort. I thought I was happy at Don Luis's Old Age Home when I didn't know it was really only an illusion of the Enchanter's.

DON QUIJOTE: No more illusions. We shall have fame and glory.

SANCHO: But now all I have are the black 'n blue of bruises and a nosebleed. A nosebleed and me with no handkerchief but a sleeve.

DON QUIJOTE: Yes, I remember the battle of the dungeon well. What a conflict, what heroism against fantastic odds. At one time I was fighting forty of the Enchanter's best men.

SANCHO: There were only three.

DON QUIJOTE: Sancho, when recounting a tale of valor, the numbers make a difference. Well no matter, did you notice the way they were cowering at my noble power, and you fought so bravely; we both made Spain proud of us today. So what of a few bruises when it's fame we seek?

SANCHO: And what of the flame of that woman's teeth? That woman, even as she was biting me, kept saying that she was a barmaid earning a living. She said the only aid she was asking was money.

DON QUIJOTE: Once again, we saw the strange workings of the Enchanter. Sancho, did you not realize that that woman was no common barmaid but a princess?

SANCHO: But why did she bite me?

DON QUIJOTE: Oh, if only you had read more about the world as I have, then you could recognize the ambivalence of woman. Look Sancho, of a woman at her own wedding cries for joy then why shouldn't a woman, at her rescue from kidnap—why shouldn't she bite for happiness?

SANCHO: Then there was that man who arreared to be a bartender.

DON QUIJOTE: The word is *appeared*, you know if you read some good romantic novels you might develop an educated manner.

SANCHO: I don't need an education to know that man hit me with a bottle.

DON QUIJOTE: That man was none other than the Black Baron of Toledo, and he is notorious for his assaults against children, women and cattle.

SANCHO: Oh, so that's who he was. And he wore perfume. I remember smelling it before the bottle broke on my head and I collapsed.

DON QUIJOTE: Enough of that villain, his name shall be forgotten by history while ours will be the source of epics.

SANCHO: Yes, even I've forgotten it.

DON QUIJOTE: Now here is an apple to eat.
(He throws Sancho an apple, which Sancho eagerly devours.)
(There is the sound of an automobile in the distance that only Sancho hears.)

SANCHO: SeÒor, I believe that there are some people coming. Maybe I can beg a few pesos.

DON QUIJOTE: *(The Don stops eating and becomes irritated.)*
In not one chivalric novel—not one—does the Squire of a famous knight errant ever beg. Sancho, don't you know that it is below your dignity?

SANCHO: It is you who have read all the books. I cannot even read. I do not know what squires are supposed to do. All I know is that I am a poor man and a poor man has no dignity, only poverty. I will beg to become rich and later I shall be very dignified.
(There is the sound of muffled voices from off stage left. The Don and Sancho both notice that some people are coming down the road.)

DON QUIJOTE: Sancho, Sancho look at what is coming down this path. My bones were right and adventure is walking right into our arms.

SANCHO: What?

DON QUIJOTE: Quickly, that woman is being waylaid by that group of robbers. We must rescue her; it is our duty for God and our country. Help me up.
(Sancho helps up the Don.)

SANCHO: But SeÒor, Señor….
(The Don comes downstage in a flurry.)

DON QUIJOTE: My lance, I need my lance. Where is my lance?

(Sancho runs downstage as the Don comes upstage; they collide.)

DON QUIJOTE: Where is my lance?

SANCHO: There!

DON QUIJOTE: My horse, I must once again call upon my gallant steed Rocinante. At them Sancho, detain them until I return. Rocinante, get up. At them, Sancho, detain them until I return. Rocinante, get up gallant steed Rocinante.
(The Don exits)

Rocinante get up.
(The travelers enter and Sancho plunges at the feet of the Banker. The

Banker is carrying his wife's hatbox and Juan, the chauffeur, has the rest of the luggage. Sancho tugs on the Banker's cuff as he walks.)

LADY: I told you we needed a new car; it was always in the garage. And besides it was looking shoddy. Now we must walk to town; I hope it gets dark soon.

BANKER: Yes dear, I'm sorry dear… Juan, Juan.

JUAN: Yes SeÒor.
(He comes to attention which is a difficult posture considering all the luggage he is carrying.)

BANKER: You have only one small job in this world.

JUAN: I know SeÒor, but I am proud that it is working for so kind and generous a man…

BANKER: Enough of that for now. Didn't you ever learn how to fix cars?

JUAN: No, but I shall learn as soon as we get to town.

BANKER: Excellent suggestion. Make a note of it, Juan.

(Juan fumbles with the luggage and takes out a note pad and makes a note. During this time, Sancho's tugging has become more persistent.)

BANKER: All right, what is it?

SANCHO: Excuse me, my most honorable gentleman and Lady but I am a poor peasant who is in dire need of monetary nourishment. Could you....

BANKER: *(To wife)* This is why I loathe walking places. One just never knows what kind of riffraff wait along these paths for people like us.

(Off stage right the Don speaks.)

DON QUIJOTE: Rocinante, you are a gallant steed, please get up and act like one.

SANCHO: *(Sancho, continues tugging.)*
You see SeÒor, this was a very bad year for the crops....There was the frost and, and the locusts.

DON QUIJOTE: *(Don off stage)*
Yes, almost all of my home, La Mancha, was eaten.

BANKER: Juan, if you knew how to fix cars we wouldn't have to put up with beggars like this.

LADY: *(Laughs)* I think he's cute, in a filthy sort of way. Juan, put this beggar off the path.

(Don off stage)

DON QUIJOTE: Hold them Sancho, I'm coming.

(Juan put the luggage down and takes Sancho by his rear and puts him upstage to the side of the path. Sancho squeals as he is handled.)

(The Don rushes on stage.)

DON QUIJOTE: There is no time for Rocinante today. Good Sancho, you are fighting well.

SANCHO: Help!

DON QUIJOTE: Ah, hold villains, you cast off my squire's resistance much too lightly. But now you must answer to me. *(He walks toward the Banker)*

DON QUIJOTE: Robbers, hand back that Lady's belongings or you will answer to the wrath of Don Quijote de la Mancha.

BANKER: Walking in the country is not only tiring, it isn't safe. *(To his wife.)* I'll try to speak to him dear. My kind sir, you say you are a knight.

DON QUIJOTE: The most famous knight-errant that the world shall ever see.

BANKER: Good, good. Then if you are a knight, I ask you as one gentleman to another, to please not walk around the countryside in your underwear, and to please not block the path I'm walking on.

DON QUIJOTE: Sancho, pay no heed to their threats. I cannot be intimidated with fear and nothing can prevent Don Quijote from saving pure and innocent women from the clutches of highway thieves. If you do not return that woman's treasure chests and beg my forgiveness, I shall be forced to cut you down like the grass.

BANKER: My good man, this is quite enough. I am the President of the Bank of Seville and no one in the world can tell Don Alejandro to beg for anything.

LADY: *(Cuddly)* Alejandro.

BANKER: What!....Yes dear.

LADY: Isn't that the cutest little beard. I think it would go so well at the Board meetings and at night I could….

BANKER: Later dear. Now you, are you getting out of the way?

DON QUIJOTE: Sancho, brace yourself to repeal their assault.
(Sancho rolls into a fat little ball in anticipation)
(The Don swings his lance in a roundhouse motion.)

JUAN: Watch out, he's got a lance!

(The Banker ducks, the woman screams, and the Don goes spinning around the stage.)

DON QUIJOTE: At them, Sancho!

JUAN: *(Pounces on Sancho and jumps up and down on his stomach.)*
So that is your master.

BANKER: *(Picks himself up.)* Wait a second….There is no need for all this. We can negotiate. In fact it's all rather simple. Since I am President of the Bank of Seville I am used to conducting negotiations. Our motto is "By your will we fill our till at the trusty Bank of Seville."

DON QUIJOTE: I am not shaken with bribes. *(He attempts another roundhouse swing.)*

(The Banker sees his opportunity and hits the Don on the back with the hatbox.)

DON QUIJOTE: *(wobbles)*
What I would have suspected, a strike in the back is a dirty blow.
(He wavers and by chance happens to knock the Banker to the ground with his lance. The Lady screams and runs to her husband who is about center stage left.)

DON QUIJOTE: Now to the assistance of my outnumbered squire.
(The chauffeur sees the Don and is panicked; he runs to the Lady's ankles. The Lady is comforting her husband, and the husband is moaning.)

SANCHO: At last. I am so faint from all the tormenting and bouncing. Thank God for the protection he has naturally given me. *(Hands on stomach.)* Oh, I am going to be sick.

DON QUIJOTE: It's all right Sancho and don't worry about my wound. It is a hazard that all knights errant must expect.

SANCHO: Wound? You have been hurt, too, my Lord?

DON QUIJOTE: It is only a mallet bash in the shoulder. But I made that coward pay for my ounce of blood with a pint of his. The scars that we have received today will be our marks of pride tomorrow. Remember Sancho: that it is only the good who ever triumph and they must always be hurt some if they are to succeed.

SANCHO: What wound, SeÒor? I can hardly see anything. If anyone's wounds should be remembered I think that they will be mine because I don't believe I shall ever get over them.

DON QUIJOTE: Nonsense Sancho. There is no sense in comparing our pains. Besides we have too much to be thankful for. Today, we have had our greatest adventure yet. It is a shame that Rocinante is too tired, but there will be other battles and I shall save her strength for those. *(Sigh)*
As for now, I am very tired; so much excitement though rewarding for the spirit is wearing on the body.
(The Don goes to sit on the hill, stage right.)

LADY: Now Juan, quickly before he tries to rescue me again.
(They pull the moaning man off the stage.)

BANKER: *(Groggy)* If cars don't work anymore we will buy a plane. I'll deduct it from my income tax. Never will I walk through a path again. Make a note, Juan.

(Juan puts him down to make the note, as the Banker moans. They go off stage left and the Banker speaks to Juan.)

BANKER: The luggage Juan.
(Juan sneaks back on stage to retrieve the luggage.)

SANCHO: SeÒor, is it true that when a knight and his squire fight bravely, that squire can ask a favor of his knight?

DON QUIJOTE: So it is written in all the best chivalric novels.

SANCHO: SeÒor, can I ask a favor?
(He kneels.)

DON QUIJOTE: Ah Sancho, my faithful friend, I see that even without the gift of literacy you have learned much. What favor do you ask of me?

SANCHO: That robber wore a very fine suit of clothes. Couldn't I trade my clothes for his, just so he looks more like a robber?

DON QUIJOTE: Hmm, let me think. You know it isn't always easy to make decisions of this sort. There are many old and ancient traditions that as a knight I am sworn to preserve.

SANCHO: Why worry about traditions, we have won, there is no need to hesitate in victory.

DON QUIJOTE: Yes Sancho, this has certainly been a day of triumph after triumph, but I didn't realize that you were also so well aware of it. But there is an ancient code to be considered.

SANCHO: If you beg my pardon SeÒor, but it is not a code I am asking but clothes.

DON QUIJOTE: I know Sancho. Now Armis de Gaul had a very good squire. For his gallantry, he awarded him a donkey tail, which he hung from his belt till he died.

SANCHO: I would look much better in a jacket, I think.

DON QUIJOTE: Yes, that's it. Lumbardio the Magnificent gave his squire a rare packet of flower seeds.

SANCHO: Flowers?

DON QUIJOTE: No, somehow I don't believe that is a fitting reward for you. But there is no precedent to give you a jacket by, but I recognize that you deserve something for your momentous day's glory.

SANCHO: Oh, oh SeÒor, you are much too kind for my little bit of assistance.

DON QUIJOTE: I think I shall take a short nap.

SANCHO: Yes, SeÒor.

DON QUIJOTE: What do you want now?

SANCHO: You were telling me about a little bit of assistance.

DON QUIJOTE: Yes....oh yes. I shall give you 50 pieces of gold. Now I shall go to sleep.

SANCHO: I am so excited, my lord. I could throw myself at your feet. *(He does.)* I could kiss every one of your toes.

DON QUIJOTE: You needn't be that excited about it, Sancho.

SANCHO: I am so happy. I knew that being your squire would become a glorious and rewarding job. I am so humble I do not even know the words to say. Except, when do I receive it.

DON QUIJOTE: What?

SANCHO: My reward.

DON QUIJOTE: Oh, yes for your little bit of assistance. You know that now you are almost a rich man. I have already promised you a kingdom; and now I am promising to you almost a king's treasure. With so many assets you can now well afford to be more patient. Patience is a virtue, Sancho.

SANCHO: If I had just 25 pesos now, I'm sure that virtue could make me as patient as anyone until I receive the rest.

DON QUIJOTE: Somehow, I believe that victory is going to your head. One must watch out for cups that runneth over. Now I shall take my nap and under no circumstances should you allow anything to disturb me. My wounds need resting.

SANCHO: *(To himself.)*
Oh what a low life I had as only a hospital attendant. It was a happy day that I helped the Don escape from the Enchanter at the Old Age Home....No, it is called a fortified old age castle, that's it. Now I have riches and soon I shall be a king and rule in rural splendor. Land and people shall bow at my feet. What treasures I'll have. Where shall I keep it? I'll have an underground cave. Yes, and there will only be one key, which I shall wear around my neck. I'll have it made to look like a cross to fool any

robbers. I just hope that the Enchanter leaves me alone.
(There is a howl.)

SANCHO: I heard a noise.

DON QUIJOTE: By the grace of God, Sancho; a mere leaf can scare your pants green.
(Another howl.)

SANCHO: That was it. I did hear it.

DON QUIJOTE: It's probably lovers….let me sleep.

SANCHO: But it was horrible. I am scared, SeÒor.

DON QUIJOTE: You are right Sancho. There is no telling what strange adventure lurks for us. It might even be another trick of the Enchanter's. We must take precautions. I'll sleep with my lance nearby and you keep watch to make sure we do not suffer a surprise attack.

(FATERIO appears. He is old and ragged and comes from a cave in the rocks. He has been running wild in the mountains for years. He has a beard and staff.)

SANCHO: God help me, your poor and loyal servant Sancho calls upon you.

DON QUIJOTE: Stay back whatever you are. I am the mighty Don Quijote. If you are a friend you will be welcome but if a foe you will be beaten.

(FATERIO walks between them, mumbling "Ehs".)

SANCHO: My Lord. Oh my Lord, I shall remember to eat fish on every Friday. I will eat fish on every day, only please save me.

FATERIO Eh . . . Such a noble stance;
And mighty lance.
You must be a knight of course, of course.
And a horse, you have a horse.

DON QUIJOTE: My horse is the bravest stallion in all of Spain. She charges like the wind and gallops like the waves.

FATERIO: Of course, of course, what a horse.
I knew a knight once.
That knight was very bright,
But his friend was very dounce.
I also knew a girl,
She would always seem
Like my last night's dream.
Always, always, always.

(Sancho stops praying and goes to the Don.)

DON QUIJOTE: Yes, I also have a Lady. I know what you feel. My Lady is the Dulcinea del Torboso and she is the most beautiful woman on earth. As a knight, I am sworn to defend her against assaulters, trickery, or dragons or anything that might harm herself or her reputation. Sancho, stop holding on to me.

SANCHO: But SeÒor, look how he is dressed, you can tell a man by his clothes. I am scared.

DON QUIJOTE: Come fellow protector of a Lady, speak with us. You must have many interesting adventures to tell. What is your name?

FATERIO: *(Charges at them.)*
Faterio is my name. Do you look for me by name?

SANCHO: I am so scared I cannot even remain quiet. SeÒor Faterio, you are speaking to the famous knight Don Quijote de la Mancha and I warn you that he has fear of nothing. And I am his squire, Sancho Panza, and I have fear of everything. Please, please go away, if not for your sake then my preservation.

DON QUIJOTE: Sancho please try to control your timidity because it is getting in the way of our adventures. The steadfast must be strong.

SANCHO: I am too scared to move.

FATERIO Do you hunt me?
If so then I flee.
Like before, long before;
She was rich and I so poor.
She so beautiful;
And I unsuitable.
Then there was he so well bred
And me so underfed.
Hunt me,
I flee;
Rich poor,
Me no more.

SANCHO: Maybe we should flee too.

DON QUIJOTE: Teaching you how to be valiant isn't easy. In all the best chivalric novels is some rhyme; one does well to listen because he can learn so much. Faterio, please continue. We mean you no harm.

FATERIO Harm,
Then I flee.
Years and years and never let me.
Oh harm,
such alarm for me.
Just for She.

But not of He.

SANCHO: I don't understand.

DON QUIJOTE: I admit that sometimes the poetic communication is not the easiest, but concentrate. Faterio, Faterio, do you think that you might….

FATERIO On her wedding night….

SANCHO: Now I am understanding.

DON QUIJOTE: Well at least there are some illusions you are able to recognize.

FATERIO On her wedding night.
I raised my might.
With a dagger I caused Him fright.

DON QUIJOTE: Me,
Flee,
Chase me,
No let me be,
You, you who never me rest,
Don't you think that plan the best.
Never, never, never.

DON QUIJOTE: Sancho, be on your guard, this Faterio may be either a trick or a victim of the Enchanter.

SANCHO: No, not the Enchanter again; he never lets us rest.

FATERIO Amidst the cakes and pigs on spits,
Right up to where that robber-Banker sits.
I have come I screamed,
Sit down he beamed.

SANCHO: A feast.

FATERIO No, I said,
I'm not misled,
When it is she you led
From my bed.

SANCHO: Go on, continue, this is an interesting adventure.

FATERIO Wait, wait he said,
Then by his sly knife how quickly I bleed;
Then the feast become still
And my love wailed a shrill
And she between us plunged
Just as my dagger lunged….
It was my knife, my knife;
I killed my dream and ruined my life.
I killed my dream and ruined my life.
(Faterio starts to exit.)
Watch the harm, there is alarm.
(He howls as he leaves.)

SANCHO: SeÒor, he lives inside those rocks. I think he has probably been there for years. He must live in a cave.

DON QUIJOTE: An excellent deduction.

SANCHO: Those caves are very damp and smelly; but then you don't have to pay any rent. SeÒr, what is the matter?

DON QUIJOTE: Nothing, nothing.

SANCHO: Are your wounds hurting you again? Maybe that backrub would help.

DON QUIJOTE: No thank you Sancho, I am just thinking about Faterio.

SANCHO: Do you think the Enchanter sent him here to scare us?

DON QUIJOTE: Nothing scares Don Quijote de la Mancha. I am the bravest knight in the world. It is just that that tale was so strange.

SANCHO: Yes, the story was almost as strange as his name. I believe that your friend was even more strange. There were many like him in the Old Age Home of Don Luis.

DON QUIJOTE: Remember Sancho, that castle that we were imprisoned in only seemed to be what it wasn't and all those people you speak of were victims of the Enchanter. The Enchanter works in very strange and mysterious ways; he makes people seem to be what they are not. And now I shall take that nap that I need so much. The rest will do both my wounds and age some good.

SANCHO: Excuse me SeÒor, but before you go to sleep could you tell me some more about my kingdom? Just the thought of my kingdom makes me happy.

DON QUIJOTE: Yes, of course Sancho.

SANCHO: Will it have trees?

DON QUIJOTE: Not trees Sancho but forests. It will be filled with forests and lakes and streams.

SANCHO: What will the land be like?

DON QUIJOTE: The land shall be so fertile that where someone drops a pit a plant will bloom.

SANCHO: Will it have a castle?

DON QUIJOTE: Did you ever hear of a kingdom without a castle?

SANCHO: I should have known. I bet it will have at least 10 rooms.

DON QUIJOTE: Not 10—a hundred, Sancho! And there will be a huge ballroom for you to entertain your guests, a kitchen filled with the world's best foods and rooms filled with beds.

SANCHO: And thick, thick mattresses, oh I can't wait. It all seems almost like a wonderful dream.

DON QUIJOTE: It will not be long. We just have to become a little more famous first.

SANCHO: *(Sancho has been pacing up and down.)*
SeÒor . . .

DON QUIJOTE: Why are you pacing?

SANCHO: I have to. I have to….Always after I eat an apple I have to….

DON QUIJOTE: Out with it, well it must be your modesty. One mustn't be so ashamed of the natural ways of nature.

SANCHO: I must go, SeÒor....I'll be sick soon.
(Exit, very constipatedly Sancho.)

DON QUIJOTE: Now for my rest. Sancho is a wonderful squire but he is always asking me about his kingdom. From the way he has been acting lately, I don't think he shall ever be satisfied. But now for some sleep . . .

(There is a pause as Don goes to sleep; but this time the lights are a little lower as dusk begins to fall.)

(Enter Diablo in a puff of smoke. Diablo is young and wearing a three button-down suit. He has an obvious false mustache and goatee. He is carrying a miniature lance.)

DON QUIJOTE: *(Is awakened.)* No, not another. I guess a knight must expect adventures but can I never rest?

DIABLO: Hey SeÒor Don Quijote, Don Quijote de la Mancha.

DON QUIJOTE: He knows my name. Who is it that disturbs me from my sleep? If you know my name then you must also know that by rudely awakening me I might have maimed or murdered you in my fury.

DIABLO: Oh, come now Quijote.

DON QUIJOTE: You seem to be another knight, yet not just another knight. I shall control my rage so that you can tell me what you want.

DIABLO: I have waited a very long time for this moment.

DON QUIJOTE: Tell me your name and pay homage to me. I am the world's most famous knight errant. If you do not tell me your name….

DIABLO: My name is Diablo, Diablo!

DON QUIJOTE: This has been a day of strange names. What do you want with me?

DIABLO: Old man, you knew I would come. We both knew it, didn't we?

DON QUIJOTE: I don't know why you have come but I am the bravest knight in the world and I have never been afraid of anything.

DIABLO: If you haven't then I think that now is the appropriate time to be, but you really are even without my efforts.

DON QUIJOTE: Enough. Tell me where you are from.

DIABLO: I am from the place where dreams grow cold and excitement weary. I have come for you, SeÒor.

DON QUIJOTE: No, you shall never take me to a place like that. Defend yourself. If need be, I shall battle you to the death. Don Quijote will meet any challenge.

DIABLO: Look, all of this fuss isn't necessary. You can't win you know.

DON QUIJOTE: Ah, now there you are wrong, even if you know my name you obviously have no knowledge of my exploits. I have never, I have never lost.

DIABLO: You've lost by winning.

DON QUIJOTE: Then defend yourself, for your own protection.

(The Don lunges at Diablo but cannot hit him, his lance always stops before connecting. Diablo takes a yawn and lifts his little lance and the Don goes flying backwards.)

DIABLO: Must we continue further with this nonsense, though I admit I like the costume. You know, I have never played a knight before, and now I can even play with one. OK, try not to be too upset when I tell you this but the Dulcinea del Torboso is a hag.

DON QUIJOTE: You speak my Lady's name in vain. I am a knight and I am sworn to protect her and her reputation.

DIABLO: Look, believe me Quijote, your Dulcinea has got quite a reputation without your help.

DON QUIJOTE: Your words only turn my rags into might; now prepare yourself for the end.

DIABLO: Come then, you're only making it tougher on yourself but I guess you won't be satisfied until you realize how helpless your vivid imagination is against the bitter reality of my unfailing lance.

(The Don charges like before and Diablo again points his lance at him, only this time with more energy and the Don goes flying back and onto the ground.)

DON QUIJOTE: No, no I am beaten.

DIABLO: Can't say I didn't tell you so. Now according to the ancient traditions of knights, having been beaten you are in my mercy. Have I got it right, Quijote?

DON QUIJOTE: Let me see, in the case of Dumindo when he was beaten, he was put at the mercy of his victor's feet. It was unfortunate for Dumindo because his victor proceeded to step on him.

DIABLO: I shall be more merciful. First I ask you to recant about your Lady, the one that you call the Dulcinea del Torboso.

DON QUIJOTE: Never.

DIABLO: Well, you picked a very pretty name but in Torboso she is commonly referred to as the Fishwoman. Come on, recant.

DON QUIJOTE: You should have to cut off all my limbs, leave me in the sun and stick me full of stakes and still I would not recant.

DIABLO: Oh, sometimes you make things so difficult. Some will just never listen to the cold facts of reason.
(Puts lance to the Don's throat.)
Recant!

DON QUIJOTE: No.

DIABLO: Just a little.

DON QUIJOTE: Never!

DIABLO: This is one of those days, all right, all right. I guess everything isn't necessary. Will you renounce your name and hang up your honor? That is an ancient tradition, isn't it?

DON QUIJOTE: In the case of Luzembo, he is a similar….

DIABLO: Sorry I asked. Will you never stop telling your noble knight stories? Look, you are beaten, whipped, Quijote, and now facing even death. Please try to realize how grave your circumstances are and stop your old errant memories. They are no longer fitting.

DON QUIJOTE: Yes, I am beaten. Never did I think that this day would come. What is it you want of me? Is it my name? Maybe the name of Don Quijote will bring you the same fame and countless glories that it has brought me.

DIABLO: My name has won me enough that I don't need yours. I want you to take back your old name.

DON QUIJOTE: My what?

DIABLO: There you go, forgetting it again. It's Alonso the Good.

DON QUIJOTE: But what kind of the name is that? It has no ring of power, no sound of fury.

DIABLO: Neither do you now.

DON QUIJOTE: I believe that I will be able to get used to it. Oh mighty oppressor, what other advantages do you wish to take from me?

DIABLO: Please just call me Diablo, and without some of the emotion. I want you to hang up your armor.

DON QUIJOTE: My armor. How could I? What will I wear?

DIABLO: Are you hanging it up?

DON QUIJOTE: Yes, it was getting heavy anyway. You know I am a pretty old man.

DIABLO: Yes I know.

DON QUIJOTE: Tell me Don Luis didn't send you, you're not one of those social workers.

DIABLO: No, I'm not.

(Diablo starts to exit.)

DON QUIJOTE: Then he must be, he must be . . .

DIABLO: Yes, I am the Enchanter. *(He vanishes in a puff of smoke.)*

(Enter Sancho to find the Don on the ground.)

SANCHO: I feel so good now, SeÒor. I am ready to go off again in search of new adventures. The Squire Sancho Panza and his noble Knight Don Quijote de la Mancha shall create history!

DON QUIJOTE: Alonso the Good?

SANCHO: What? You must be joking, SeÒr.

DON QUIJOTE: Call me Alonso the Good.

SANCHO: But that is not your name. That is only the name that the Enchanter gave you at Don Luis's fortified Old Age Castle.

DON QUIJOTE: Never was there such a place.

SANCHO: But you were the one who told me about it.
Yes, now I understand it all. This is just the work of the Enchanter again. He never leaves me alone. I must be careful and protect the kingdom of my interests.

DON QUIJOTE: I am going to go home to La Mancha, Sancho.

SANCHO: No, you can't. We are going to become famous. *(The Don takes off his armor.)*

What are you doing, that is your armor!

DON QUIJOTE: I have no need for it now.

SANCHO: Maybe I can use it then.

DON QUIJOTE: Yes, you can have whatever you can take, but I don't think it was made for you. But even if the suit doesn't fit you'll probably wear it. I am going to gather poor Rocinante, together we will return to our home; soil to the plow and I, and I . . .

SANCHO: Stop it Enchanter. You are ruining everything.

DON QUIJOTE: Good-bye my good friend. You have served me well. But now I must go. I'm sorry that you don't understand the reasons yet but, in time, you will. Yes we have had many good times together, but those are over now. I am old Sancho, I am too old to be a knight. I am too old to be anything except what I really am. Good-bye, my thanks, my compliments.

SANCHO: This must be some terrible dream. It cannot end this way. SeÒr, when am I to get my kingdom that I have been hoping for? SeÒr, when?
(He runs after the Don.)

THE END

SCORPIO

SCORPIO

Characters:
Stanley
Tom (Female)

Setting:

The living room in a Bronx apartment house. It is wildly and erratically decorated with old furniture, bulletin boards and burlap. One door leads to the hallway and the other to a bedroom. Surrounded by other tenements, little light comes through the window. The studio kitchen is visible; a bridge table is in the corner of the room and a phone, on a tray, is suspended from the ceiling.

Time:

The present on a hot day in the beginning of June.

At Rise:

The room is dark and a match is lit. Tom plans to light one of the six candles she has semi-

encircled herself with. Tom is a short, coldly attractive girl of about 20. Her long red hair hangs down her turquoise Chinese bathrobe. She begins to light the candle, then looks up.

TOM: Ruined it. Ruined. Never can finish. *(Listening)* Yes, I know dear, just a simple seizure.
(She puts on the light and begins putting candles in a lavishly decorated shoebox.)
I heard ya, I hear. . . Just when I begin, too. Look, Martha, I'll be right there…What I put up with, I shouldn't talk about. I'm coming.

(There is a knocking on the hallway door as Tom goes into the bedroom. The knocking increases. Stanley, who has been knocking on the door, sneaks inside the living room. He opens the hallway door cautiously. He is about 19; and always smiling; handsome; dressed neatly in a white summer suit and weighed down by a heavy black salesman's sample case. He is visually astounded by the room and its suspended telephone. As he gapes, Tom comes back in, looking for something.)

Now where is it?

(She suddenly notices Stanley and brightens.)

STANLEY: *(Somewhat stunned)*

What? . . .Miss, hello.
(She ignores him.)
I'm your . .
(She sneers.)
. . . hello, anyway, your door's not . . .

TOM: Have you got a pencil? It's for my roommate.

STANLEY: *(looking inside his coat pocket)*

TOM: She's an epileptic. *(To the bedroom door)* Just hang on Martha.

STANLEY *(Amazed)*
Oh God.
(He frantically looks through his pockets, then opens his sample case and starts taking things out, hoping to find the pencil.)
Try to keep things neat you know.

TOM: Swell!

STANLEY: Never do though.

TOM: Have you got a pencil or not?

STANLEY *(Looking)*
You want a pencil, huh?

TOM: Not very quick are you.

STANLEY: I'm trying, Miss.

TOM: Lotta good that'll do her.

STANLEY *(To Martha in the bedroom)*
Hey in there, I'm trying.
(Tom plucks the pencil from behind Stanley's ear.)

TOM Thanks.
(She starts for the bedroom)

STANLEY *(Relieved)*
Funny thing that?
(Forcing a laugh.)

TOM: No, not at all.
(Over her shoulder as she leaves.)
Hey, don't go. I might like you.

STANLEY: Oh, Miss, what's your name?
(Seeing the mess he's made of his samples, he begins to pack them and hums "Tea for Two" while shuffling about.)

TOM *(Entering the room)*
Can't have her swallowing her tongue, if you know what I mean.

STANLEY: I suppose Miss . . . I just came in here to tell you your door's not locked. I could have walked right in.

TOM *(In a teasing manner.)*

Well, well, well. What would you have taken? My lamp or virginity or something?

STANLEY: I don't believe it's safe to leave your door . . ..

TOM: And you don't have a choice, kid.

STANLEY: This is supposed to be a dangerous neighborhood.

TOM: Are you dangerous or something?
(Catching a fancy and cornering him.)
A murderer!...No, pity, might have been interesting. Don't know any….Ya mean, you walked in here to my place–it's nice, ain't it–just to tell me my door wasn't locked?

STANLEY: Yes, that's what I did, that's all.

TOM: I could've guessed it if I wanted to bother. Always happens, I know the type, kid….the kind that hangs around apartment buildings, trying all the doorknobs until BAM one of them is open. Then in you go racing through all the furniture looking for some poor defenseless girl to tell all your problems to.
(She approaches him.)

STANLEY: Well excuse me. But I don't make a habit of opening strange doorknobs nor handing out pencils. In fact, that was my only pen....

TOM: *(Cutting him off.)* Clean up, will ya.

STANLEY: *(Putting the samples back.)*
I certainly will. That's what I was doing.

TOM: The other junk too. I don't want that crap all over the floor, ruining the interior.

STANLEY: *(Noticing he's left some crumpled hats out.)*
Give me time, please. The hats. Always forget them.

TOM: No wait, will ya....
(She picks up a Dutchboy style hat and puts it on.)
Pretty groovy.

STANLEY: *(Trying to reach for it while Tom prances about it dancing).*
Miss, this is charity stuff and I'm responsible. Can you try and handle the merchandise with care. It happens to be made by the blind.

TOM: You know you can tell.
(She picks up some underwear from the case and puts it on Stanley's head as he tries to take her hat.)

STANLEY: This is not a hat. And I'm sure the blind man who made it would not be happy to hear how his handiwork has been abused.

TOM: Why knock it, it looks good on you. *(Stanley takes it off; Tom throws him the hat she's been wearing.)*

STANLEY: Now look, this is a new job and I don't want to be upset.

TOM: Sh-h-h

STANLEY: Don't sh-h-h me.

TOM: Silly. All about little blind men. *(She laughs.)*

STANLEY: It's not funny.

TOM: Yes it is and come on laugh, smiling puss. *(She chases after him, trying to get him to laugh and eventually succeeds.)*

STANLEY: It's better to laugh, isn't it?

TOM: Much better, kid.

STANLEY: Stop calling me that. What's your name?

TOM: *(Disgusted.)* A lull in the conversation....Tom. What's yours, if I may be so boring?

STANLEY: Stanley….What do you mean, your name is Tom?

TOM: Look, with a name like Stanley, you should talk.

STANLEY: My boss doesn't have any first name.

TOM: Some people don't need any….See our phones, we've got lots. One in the bathroom. It's a maroon Princess.

STANLEY: *(Looking at suspended phone)* Nice.

TOM: I am a writer.

STANLEY: Everyone should have a hobby.
(Tom gets a huge folder of articles and throws it on Stanley's lap.)

TOM: I'm editor of the school paper, the *Kumquat*. I was almost kicked out for one of my columns. Read one. Clean up later.
(He opens the folder and takes out a column; becomes interested.)
What we need here is a fishnet. A gigantic fishnet. Staple it over here, suspend it there. Wow. What an effect. Do you have a fishnet? Hey!

STANLEY: *(Looking up)* Huh….I don't think so. About this 16-year-old boy starting a nudist camp for his friends.

TOM: Sure, kids do the darndest things....A fishnet, one like the gladiators used. And with a lever so it can be dropped. Or a trident. Wow. What I could do with a trident.

STANLEY: No I don't, I'll be....

TOM: *(Looking at Stanley who has put down the column.)*
Hey, I've got a great short story about my abortion.

STANLEY: *(Pause)*
Did you really have an abortion?

TOM: *(Looking through her filing cabinet; casually.)*
It's the only thing to do when you're pregnant you know . . . Didn't mean to shock you.

STANLEY: No. *(To himself)* I guess it all comes from leaving your doors unlocked.

TOM: *(Giving up looking.)*
Someone has it. Unless Martha hid it.
(Pause) Well, it's really good. Our literary magazine, *Rampant,* refused to print, so the Newman Club decided to use it as an example for something. The Priest censored it and the whole staff quit.

STANLEY: You mean Martha hides....

TOM: *(Softly)* Ah, she's resting.
(In normal voice.)
Really a little horny, if you know what I mean. Do you like my place?

STANLEY: Do I like….

TOM: You've had enough time. I want your opinion, whatever that might be.
(Drawing towards him.)
What do you like?

STANLEY: *(Beaming.)* Your furniture!

TOM: *(Incredulous)* The furniture?

STANLEY: And the air.

TOM: My air?

STANLEY: Yup. Makes me feel….ever spend Saturdays at museums? You know, something different for a change. And it isn't cluttered with Danish Modern.

TOM: Oh….That's functional Salvation Army. Cheap. Maybe you'd like to see my bed? Don't get any creepy ideas, just see it. It's great. Wood and big; friend varnished and stained the whole thing. Cover's orange. Whole room is great. I have green and blue and red lights in it and some old chemistry test tubes hanging from the ceiling. Also a Winnie the Pooh doll; I believe they're very rare.

STANLEY: Is that where Martha is?

TOM: Yes; later then; she'd kind of screw up the effect the way she is now....I'm glad you're staying.

STANLEY: *(Rising)* I didn't mention staying.

TOM: Something about you. Your smile. That's it.

STANLEY: Wait, I've got a job.

TOM: It's kind of artistic.

STANLEY: I'm a working man, at least for the summer.

TOM: *(Seating him.)*
You were lucky. People next door would of cracked open your head with a toaster....walking in that way. Why, that's a silly thing to do. Do you like being a sales thing?

STANLEY: I need the money.

TOM: We all need that.

STANLEY: It's educational. You can find out things of interest.

TOM: Trivia, the things you learn from people in the Bronx.

STANLEY: Well, that's how I know this isn't a safe place. I've been refused entrance by at least 30 Italian-Irish-Jewish mothers in the past week. Know why? Cause this is a dangerous neighborhood. You shouldn't live here, a nice girl like you. There have been, let's see, four robberies, a few miscellaneous abductions and only yesterday, two murders of 93-year-old women; one for 32 cents and the other for 20 cents and a salami sandwich.

TOM: Shame, shame. The old ladies' bags never do have much money….You're the first salesman that's come in here. Of course, as a rule, Martha and I generally loathe salesmen.

STANLEY: I'm tired of the things I've been seeing. Days of doors. Nasty old men and mean little children. Doors that are locked when open. But not your apartment.

TOM: If you're going to start….

STANLEY: Now your apartment is something I've read about.

TOM: Yea….

STANLEY: Funny. Makes me forget all the things I'm sorry I've done and sorry I'm doing.

Like this sample case, Herman. *(He picks up his case.)* Given to people who are in need of a reason for hospitalization. My boss gave it to me.

TOM: Don't tell me about your dull job.

STANLEY: All day it's an act. You'll like it. You be the SeÒrita.
(He begins to wrap a serape around her; getting a bit tangled. Tom is confused but interested.)
Let me show you....you just come along. OK. Ka-Zam!
(He goes into a bastardized sales pitch.)
Let me show you what I've got, Señorita....Here we go. Herman and I have been out together. You can please put the hammer down now. No, I'm not ordinary, a college student. Yes, now you can lower it. I'll show you what I got. Vomit some soap, Herman.
(Taking a bar.)
Clean and simple. But I've got more, lots more. Things from the East, things from the West, things from in-between. The cheapest, the most practical, the stuff shown on TV. A carnival of pretty products for you to choose what you like....You have 11 seconds.
(Tom beings to look at the merchandise and "get into the act." Stanley looks at his watch and sings "Tick-a tocka, Tick-a-tocka.")

Time. For you, Señorita, I'd sell everything.

TOM: *(In a Spanish accent.)*
Yes, yes . . . oh, I like this and that and that . . . oh, I love this one. And especially that color; such color . . . Beautiful, I like them all.

STANLEY: My little flower, why you can buy them all!

TOM: *(Unwrapping the serape.)*
But my apologies to you and Herman, for I have money for nothing.

STANLEY: That's what I like. Heat. Bridges buckling and buildings sweating.

TOM: *(In normal voice.)*
Then why haven't you taken off your jacket?

STANLEY: My job.

TOM: It's a lot more comfy without that on.

STANLEY: Hard getting adjusted to all those people who couldn't care less if I fell down all their staircases and had my head drop off….Selling a soul for some soapsuds.

TOM: Stanley, let me take your jacket; you can keep your soul.

STANLEY: You understand!

TOM: But I don't talk about it. God, you go on.

STANLEY: That's why, well, when I came in here, it wasn't hot.

TOM: We have a fan.

STANLEY: Wanted to tell someone….

TOM: Ah-ha!

STANLEY: *(Hurt.)* You know what I meant.

TOM: *(Flippantly.)*
Heat it all the time. Hung-up people always happen here. Float-in; float-out.

STANLEY: It's good to talk to someone. . .

TOM: You've got problems, huh. Mother's on your ass. Well, I know all about it.

STANLEY: *(Packing up his suitcase.)*
Forget it….
(Shouting.)
I'll leave, it'll make things easier.
(The suitcase opens and everything falls out.)

TOM: Sure you will.

STANLEY: *(A bit discouraged.)*

Do you want me to prove it? To walk right out of here and show you I would leave?

TOM: Ah, too emotional. If you were leaving you wouldn't be telling me. Emotional people never say what they're going to do, they only remember afterwards.

STANLEY: *(Calming down.)*
Felt like shouting, that job.

TOM: *(Maternally.)*
You've just got some problems; so does Martha, so do we all.

STANLEY: Words, words. A tea-kettle of syllables wanting to shriek.

TOM: Well, better to learn how to digest your words. They can't do much damage in your stomach.

STANLEY: I've wanted to yell since I started this job.

TOM: What you want now is a Coke.

STANLEY: I don't like….

TOM: With coconut rum. Just relax and take off your things.
(She goes to the studio kitchen to fix the drinks.)

I don't want you to go. There aren't many smiles around here. Not real smiles; just alcoholic smiles from the people who like to ride with the top down because they think it has sex appeal. . . Do you have one?

STANLEY: My family does.

TOM: Really, Stanley has a convertible. Tom likes convertibles too.
(To the bedroom door.)
Keep resting until all the trembles stop.
(Handing him the drink.)
Stanley, take Tom for a drive.
(She sucks her thumb and Stanley nods approval)
Then let's toast to it....And to madness. Sip it.

STANLEY: To Lewis Carroll, I like him....I'm feeling OK. Shouldn't we bash the glasses against the kitchen cabinet or something?

TOM: Only when we use paper cups.

STANLEY: Good. I'm forgetting that job. And my home, that's where I'm living for the summer. A house full of empty rocking horses.

TOM: Don't ruin it. Talking about parents and parking tickets. Not after Lewis Carroll, will ya. Or the complexes. Everybody talks about Oedipus and Electra and they never read the plays.

STANLEY: I don't like talking about them either.

TOM: The bores do. Never know whether to call them Mother or Dad, Father or Mom.

STANLEY: Mine live in Queens. During school I'm away.

TOM: They can't understand you.

STANLEY: They got me this job.

TOM: Sure, mother's on your ass.

STANLEY: *(Getting angry.)*

TOM: All those people with their unzipped flies and baloney sandwiches, cartoon people, growing up into these people outside. Making money and starting to worry about making money and sitting down on Sunday nights to plan a proper life as if they could ever get it then or enough of it to last them through the week.

STANLEY: Well, sometimes parents plan too much.

TOM: *(Accusing him.)*
You've been put in an envelope; and then suddenly wonder if you mind licking stamps.... *(picks up a comic book)* See this comic; not a real comic, a satire on

them. Cartoons laughing at other cartoons. But so many people read these as if they were Donald Duck or something. They don't even get the goddamn joke. And that's really the laugh.
(She tears it in half.)

STANLEY: You shouldn't get yourself so excited about comic books.

TOM: I wonder if you get the joke?

STANLEY: Me?

TOM: Yea man, smiles not included, you're just another little boy who keeps his hands under the covers so no one will snap it off. Same problems, same people. Tired of it. Give me something. Something exciting, to grab me by the hair and carry me into the wind. I love storms, standing out in them. Something….Nothing makes me happier than hurricanes.

STANLEY: What can I do?
(Shouting.)
I just came in to tell you about your crummy door. And you don't have to yell.

TOM: Sure, sure….a hope once. A dream that didn't work.

STANLEY: No I yelled again. I'm usually quiet.

TOM: Who knows what usual means?

STANLEY: But I'm glad, glad I did it. It felt good.

TOM: Oh brother.

STANLEY: I yelled because I think I care about you and.....

TOM: Don't be a drag.

STANLEY: I know I don't know you but with a little time, and we could go for a ride and....

TOM: That's stupid.

STANLEY: Stupid.

TOM: Especially when I'm being stupid. Two people should never be stupid together....It's a rule....I was right about your smile. It can't be excluded.
(Looks at Stanley's wristwatch.)
Anyway it's time for Martha's apple.
(To the bedroom.)
Hold on, dear. Be patient.

STANLEY: How's she going to eat it? She's still got my pencil.

TOM: She likes to hold them.
(Stanley looks at his watch while Tom throws an apple into the bedroom)
Heads up, Martha.

STANLEY: I should have refused this Coke.

TOM: I meant to tell you about that stuff, you're too polite. Normally, you wouldn't have gotten the drink. Polite people seldom get the things they want, you know.

STANLEY: But I still can't help feeling that I should be out there, knocking on the doors.

TOM: If you start complaining about your job again, we'll talk out in the hallway, so you don't get a guilt complex.
(Stanley looks at his watch.)

STANLEY: So Martha just holds them, eh?

TOM: What?

STANLEY: Her apples.

TOM: Yea…ever since she was married. Had it annulled; he turned out to be a creep.
(Stanley looks at his watch again.)
Stop it. I was telling you about . . .

STANLEY: I'm listening.

TOM: Look at these. *(She shows him a long set of fingernails.)*
Aren't they a prize? And you wouldn't want me to scratch you.

STANLEY: I was only seeing if it was working. They break frequently.

TOM: I scratch the bores. Try not to be next. For Martha's sake, she hates blood, it makes her convulse. I'd better get my button. It was made for my birthday by....especially for me. It's big....my button. Where did she put it?
(Tom looks around the room.)

STANLEY: What are you looking for?

TOM: *(Looking under the sofa cushion on which he is sitting.)*
My button, you've got to see it before....Hey, great!
(She pulls out the button.) It says: SEX AND DESTRUCTION, in red letters.)

STANLEY: That's what you've been looking for?

TOM: You've got to see it before....

STANLEY: Do you often go around wearing that?

TOM: Why not? It was made for my birthday. I'm a Scorpio.

STANLEY: I'm a Gemini. I don't get buttons because of it.

TOM: And I've got red hair....This happens to mean something; I wanted to show it to you . . .

STANLEY: *(Reading it.)*
Sex and destruction.
(He takes a sip of his drink.)

TOM: Pooh. Can't say I didn't try, can you Stanley, can you?
(He picks up his cup to put it in the sink.)
Poor adventureless, Stanley? But you've still got some time to learn.

STANLEY: Not much. I've still a quota to make.

TOM: *(Stanley bringing glasses to sink.)*
Put those down.

STANLEY: Helping.

TOM: I didn't ask for any.

STANLEY: I don't mind. At home I never do them.

TOM: I mind.
(She takes the glasses away from him.)

STANLEY: I take out the garbage when I remember.

TOM: Don't need people wandering in here to give a helping hand with the housework. Understand.

STANLEY: Wanted to show you....

TOM: Martha does them.
(Tom drops them into the sink.)

Makes her feel good.

STANLEY: I, I.....I thought you were going to tell me about her.

TOM: All right….It was after her marriage, that was when she was 17, that the fits first began.
(Fingering his coat.)
Will you take that off now.

STANLEY: You were telling me…..

TOM: Go no sleeves or something, Stanley. Don't be embarrassed. My friend Timothy used to be ashamed that he had no sleeves; then he met some guy who hadn't any buttons . . . that's when he became a Yogi.

STANLEY: *(Tom takes off his jacket for him and Stanley becomes flustered.)*
Only because it's a suit and the jacket goes with the pants. Water. Do you think I could have some….

TOM: Coke. Now you're comfy.

STANLEY: I don't like Coke. It's bad for the teeth.

TOM: You're not supposed to chew it. Before….

STANLEY: I would have preferred if you asked me to have a glass of water with you.

TOM: Sentimental. It takes guts to refuse a Coke?

STANLEY: My jacket.

TOM: Don't get emotional and want to leave or do the dishes or something. We're starting to learn about each other.

STANLEY: I'd feel better if . . .

TOM: You can hold it, but don't put it on.

STANLEY: It's not often that I wear a suit . . .

TOM: All my friends come in here and do what they want.

STANLEY: *(A pause.)*
Run around ripping their jackets off?

TOM: Not all my friends; hardly know them; isn't it exciting?

STANLEY: You mean you let a bunch of strangers rush in here....

TOM: Martha invites them all. Went to a film last week and brought back 13.

STANLEY: She's very hospitable.

TOM: She's a good journalist. Why don't you write for a paper?

STANLEY: I don't think ours is like yours. Anyway, I detest newspapers. Know why?

TOM: Yes, another lull in the conversation.

STANLEY: 'Cause the whole world's identical to these customers in the Bronx.

TOM: Doesn't concern, doesn't concern, no, no, no.

STANLEY: Don't you know about it? And my job reminds me of it all.

TOM: OK. Tell me Stanley, who do I really care gets bombed as long as I don't get bombed.

STANLEY: Who?....so then you'd care.

TOM: Then there's no use. You don't care because your caring can't do anything.

STANLEY: I want to try.

TOM: You'll learn.

STANLEY: I've always believed in trying.

TOM: And failing? Have you always believed in that? And if you don't, right off that is, you can't beat them all. There's a hell of rotten people out there. You've at least learned that.

STANLEY: The doors outside....

TOM: That's what you've been yelling about, isn't it.

STANLEY: I wanted to tell....noisy pounding.....I don't think I can continue beating them.

TOM: You can't even beat them down....Unless, you want your hands all bloody like Lady MacBeth....I love Lady MacBeth....She's cool, you know really cool. With her washing hands is an experience, you don't just go to the goddamn sink and get clean....There's nothing that makes me happy as a good tragedy.

STANLEY: I like happy endings with smiles.

TOM: There's only one ending.

STANLEY: It doesn't have to be without smiles.

TOM: I don't want to talk about that any more. You're going to sit here and smoke?

STANLEY: Use to smoke; quit three times.

TOM: It's going to turn you on; loosen you up. Put blood through your veins. Pot. Know what it is?

STANLEY: Pot?....Read about it.

TOM: Good. You'd like some?

STANLEY: Fits rights in with the place, doesn't it? You know, I've always wanted to try….once.

TOM: *(Getting it.)*
I'll bet. Stanley from Queens has always wanted to but didn't. Glad you're here.

STANLEY: *(Tom has a thin-looking cigarette in her mouth.)*
Is that it? Doesn't look like it.

TOM: Why does everyone who doesn't smoke pot always think it looks like something else?
(She lights up.)

STANLEY: The tobacco is all….

TOM: Martha rolls them like this. A bit sloppy. This is called a joint. Want to write that one down?
(She inhales deeply and holds the smoke down, at times covering her nose so the smoke won't escape.)

STANLEY: You're going to squash your nose.

TOM: Quiet. Keeping the smoke down. Soon Stanley, you're free. Flying on some Egyptian genie's hair…and feeling real good.

STANLEY: I don't think I'm feeling bad.

TOM: You'll feel better.
(She sucks in on the joint, hungrily.)

STANLEY: If this were in my report my boss would fire me.

TOM: Not afraid of anything. Letting your mind ride on a Ferris wheel until all of a sudden you're on top of it and you can look down and see what's left of you revolving, revolving.

STANLEY: And he'd tell my parents. They'd fire me too if I weren't related.

TOM: Now do you want some?

STANLEY: *(Hoping)*
It's dangerous a little.

TOM: You've got to take what adventure you can get in the Bronx.

STANLEY: I love adventurers.

TOM: What about you? Haven't you got guts?

STANLEY: I've got them.

TOM: Well, they're not exactly falling out of your stomach.

STANLEY: I'm deciding.

TOM: And when you're high, you build your own void to play in. Fill it with some mountain springs.

STANLEY: *(to himself)*
Let them all fire me.

TOM: Decided. This isn't the legislature.

STANLEY: Yes, yes. I'd like to try. Just once.

TOM: *(Handing him another joint.)*
Your convertible will be proud.
(She lights it for him.)
One joint should be enough. Now, hold it down. Not like smoking a cigarette. Let yourself go.
(Stanley tries very hard to smoke. In his first attempts he doesn't hold the smoke down long enough. Tom takes quick drags on what is left of her joint.)
My friend Timothy the guru is also a pusher. Sells this stuff from here and saves the best….Yummy, yummy.

STANLEY: How am I doing?

TOM: Down longer. Got to feel its warmth inside you.
(Stanley tries again. This time nervously pacing the room.)

We smoke then Timothy tells some slick Buddhist parables and we sit back and discuss the Kama Sutra.

STANLEY: I did it. I did it?
(Tom shows him how and he watches her. Stanley then goes all out to hold it down. But doing it incorrectly and comically, he is quite a sight trying to stop smoke from coming out of his nose and mouth.

TOM: *(Speaking slowly and in-between drags.)* The Kama Sutra is a something book. And India's another thing. Statues of cows and people of straw. I can see it now. Only I have trouble getting to Siddhartha. Stanley you can let go now. Need something stronger for him. Stanley let go. Stanley let go now.

(She pries his hands from his nose and Stanley falls down, gasping for air.)

STANLEY: I don't think I, I feel anything.

TOM: It's not instantaneous.

STANLEY: I was trying.

TOM: Too hard.

STANLEY: I'll strangle if I take any more.
(He looks at his watch. Both he and she are feeling some of the effects.)

Funny. What if the numbers were names.
I finished my quota at Steven to James.
(Tom looks at the watch and giggles.)

TOM: We are going to need a tape recorder, I can tell.

STANLEY: Yes.

TOM: Where is it? Look.
(Tom goes to the refrigerator; Stanley looks under the sofa cushion then he crawls under the sofa.)

STANLEY: Not here, but who cares.

TOM: *(Sitting on the sofa.)*
Who cares? I don't have a tape recorder.
(She notices Stanley's feet sticking out from under the sofa.)
Two limbs of a tree.
(She tries to unlace his shoes. Stanley pulls himself from out of the sofa and comes up behind it)
I must have those.

STANLEY: No, they couldn't walk without me.

TOM: *(Crawling under the sofa.)*
I must, I must. Who says I can't? I'm a Scorpio.

STANLEY: There are no more autumn leaves; the trees have all been killed by the shadows of tall buildings.

TOM: Give me your shoes! Give me your shoes!

STANLEY: If I have but one pair to wear, then let me wear them for life . . . We need a flag. Must have a flag.
(He takes her button and attaches it to the suspended phone.)
That'll do.

TOM: These shoes are for my gladiator; the one who will slash through the fishnet.

STANLEY: *(In double-time says the American "Pledge of Allegiance" to the telephone, while Tom tries to unlace his shoes and take them off.)*

TOM: So that there will finally be something solid to stand on.

STANLEY: *(Lacing his shoes.)*
With these hands I make my own world secure in its responsibility never to leave loose ends.

TOM: And with these, I scratch your responsibilities.

STANLEY: *(Holds both of her hands together easily restraining her. He is dazed and begins to come out of it.)*
Tom.

TOM: My hair is red. *(He easily puts her hands to her sides.)*
Wow.

STANLEY: I was feeling . . . .

TOM: Great. What you just did. Strong. How come you're so . . .

STANLEY: Funny stuff.

TOM: So strong. Powerful.

STANLEY: *(Elated)* Do you think so? I want very much to be your friend.

TOM: You're OK, ya know. Not one of those mathematical midgets. The people you can count, but can't count on. People like that, the outside ones, they lock me in. Like your doors, Stanley's goddamn doors. Open all the doors in the world.

STANLEY: Yes.

TOM: You could use your strength and break every door down. Like a Goliath or something good. Then we'd skip right over them. Stanley and Tom hopping over a sea of broken doors. Hair wet in rain.

STANLEY: *(Tom starts sucking her thumb with excitement.)*
What do you eat your finger for?

TOM: There's a hell-of-a-lot in sucking your thumb.

STANLEY: It'll ruin your teeth.

TOM: Have you got some kind of dental fixation?

STANLEY: Learned about it at home.

TOM: *(Pressuring him.)*
Sure Stanley's home: Stanley?

STANLEY: It's hot in here.

TOM: *(Nagging)*
Stanley, Stanley please take out the garbage; it's good for your teeth.

STANLEY: *(Going to the window.)*Open the window more . . .
(Looking out.) There's someone across the way.

TOM: *(Standing on the sofa.)*
The house of urchins. And the wife beater.

STANLEY: He's looking right over here. He's looking at me.
(He ducks under the sill.)

TOM: With his big flat nose.

STANLEY: It's pressed against the window. He's on a stool.... Better close the blinds so he can't look in.
(The blinds come down; they are striped.)

TOM: I warned him last time.
(She opens the blinds.)

STANLEY: Now there's two of them.

TOM: The uglier one is his wife. Their TV's probably not working again.

STANLEY: *(Drawing the blinds again.)*
Now they can't look in.

TOM: *(Raising the blinds completely.)*
Relax your nerves.

STANLEY: People looking right in here.

TOM: Time for the Exasperator, Martha, Martha, old blunt nose and fat face are at it again. Get out the Exasperator!

STANLEY: *(As Tom goes into the bedroom.)*
Shouldn't I just close the blinds?
(Tom enters the room carrying a large pasteboard arm. The arm is attached to a wooden block and the middle finger is extended. She whistles a march.)
The Exasperator!

TOM: *(Putting it in the window.)*
Martha thought this up, she's beautiful.

STANLEY: *(to the bedroom door)*
Why don't you invite her in?

TOM: Sh-h-h-h-h. Wouldn't want her to crush her apples. But now I feel good. You?

STANLEY: All right.

TOM: And I want to do something creative.

STANLEY: Creative?

TOM: I want to paint.

STANLEY: *(Looking at his watch.)*Who's got time.

TOM: And after smoking. Don't you want to release yourself?

STANLEY: *(Thinking of leaving.)*
Yes. . . I don't know how to paint.

TOM: You don't have to, we'll action paint. Hang the table up.
(She goes into the studio kitchen area and begins getting mustard, eggs, black paint, ketchup, strawberry jam.)

STANLEY: Hang what up?

TOM: *(Pointing to the bridge table.)*
The table on the nail. I'll get the ingredients.

STANLEY: *(Folds back the legs and takes the table to the wall. Tom hums in the kitchen. Stanley hangs the table up and reveals a painting on the face of it. It is an abstracted nude reclining. To himself.)*
Wonderful.

TOM: Now get the board. I'll help move the furniture.
(Stanley brings out the board and he and Tom reorganize the furniture to get themselves plenty of room.)

STANLEY: *(Noticing the stuff.)*
Are those the ingredients?

TOM: We need color, Stanley; this isn't a studio. And a record. Music. Put on the album.
(Stanley puts on the album; it is a fast rock 'n' roll instrumental. Tom begins to undulate in time.)
OK . . . Ya ready?

STANLEY: Ready? What do I do?

TOM: First thing, stop thinking, begin feeling. Spontaneity.
(She takes the black paint and begins to throw it at the board. First slowly but later with more speed. She lets her paint brush run rampant enough to make Stanley crudely aware that she is also trying to paint him.)

STANLEY: You're going to get all that stuff on me.

TOM: Move through space; you've been thrown off that Ferris wheel, flung out into the Universe.
(Turning) And you can see the world Stanley, spinning below you, turning, turning. Round and round over the brown meadow; past the yellow seas.

STANLEY: *(Beginning to become nervous.)*
You're going to fall off.

TOM: Stop worrying about falling, get on the damn thing . . . A comet racing through the void; avoiding all the mean meteorites. Catching on Stanley. We need color.
(She gets mustard.)
Musty yellow.
(Almost charging at Stanley.)
Sinking into the last sunset of Hawaii. Like to see that. And we need red, red.
(She races for the ketchup.)
The red drops splatter the world.
(Stanley is cornered and trembling.)

STANLEY: Tom, stop it. I don't want to paint. I don't know how, will ya.

TOM: Join in the world, Stanley.
(She charges at him with a bottle of strawberry jam. He tries to run but she catches him.)

Here. *(She puts some in his hand.)* Use it, Stanley. Flip it. Let it go. *(She takes his hand and rubs it into the painting. Soon Stanley starts to move his hand himself. He begins to become involved but violently.)*

STANLEY: This jam feels....

TOM: Squeeze it. Let's coat the doors with it. *(She jumps on his back and they both ride up and down the painting throwing jam and mushing it into it. Tom screams with joy and Stanley pants from excitement. Then she crawls under him to put the jam on.)*
There aren't any bombs in action paintings. We can be the bombs. *(She gets the eggs.)* Exploding right before our eyes.
(She throws an egg.)

STANLEY: *(Picking up some eggs.)*
Right in the middle.
(He throws.)

TOM: Action Stanley. Excitement.
(She throws. And they both begin to stalk the painting but really each other.)
Bam.
(She throws.)

STANLEY: Bam
(He throws.)

TOM: *(She falls to the floor exhausted.)*

STANLEY: *(Shutting off the record player.)*
What a mess.
(He beings to fidget each time he looks at Tom.)

TOM: A swinging swirling mess. I love it. It means something.

STANLEY: *(Trying to be funny.)*
And it's mobile; the way the ketchup slides down the mustard.

TOM: Do you feel it? The power. The world, a case history. I'll have it exhibited, in the *Kumquat* office.

STANLEY: I don't think it will last that long. What are you going to call it?

TOM: "The Bandersnatch gets Busted." Nothing else suits; absolutely nothing.

STANLEY: *(Looking out the window and then at his watch.)*
It's getting late.

TOM: Who cares?

STANLEY: I've got a job.

TOM: There are better things to do.

STANLEY: I think I have to go.

TOM: Who asked you to?

STANLEY: So much is happening and there'll be nothing left. Just Herman, the doors and boredom.

TOM: So you're bored.

STANLEY: *(Nervously)*
I didn't mean that. What did you want me to say?

TOM: Nothing . . . That's the problem, you talked. Had a good time and now you want to find out if I'm good too.

STANLEY: Who said that?

TOM: Well, I am. And there's a number of notches on this . . .
(She points to the bulletin board.)
And any one of them would be glad to vouch for me.

STANLEY: *(Looking at the board.)*
All full of notches. . . A pornographic bulletin board.

TOM: Only the top part; bottom's Martha's; she's winning.
(Stanley starts to fix up his case again.)
I've been wondering whether or not you've got hair on your chest.

STANLEY: Can you stop. No, no I don't but I'm going to get some. I'll buy some follicle accelerator.

TOM: *(Sincerely.)*
Don't be mad with Tom.

STANLEY: *(Angry.)*
I'm not.

TOM: You're not smiling.

STANLEY: *(Forcing one.)*
Better?

TOM: Keep it. You're a hell-of-a-lot pleasanter to look at.

STANLEY: Look at the sky outside. I'm just afraid it's going to rain.

TOM: Is that all?

STANLEY: If it rains I won't be able to go. I get worried about things like that.
(Turning quickly towards the bedroom.)
And what's with her anyway? She never comes out.

TOM: Stop getting emotional.

STANLEY: But the clouds are dark now; look at them all heavy with rain. Waiting.

TOM: You're disgusted about something.

STANLEY: I don't want it to rain.

TOM: You look kind of nauseous when you're disgusted.

STANLEY: Not in the Bronx, not when I've got to go from building to building without an umbrella; not when I'm wearing a suit.

TOM: But you don't have to feel bad. If it rains, you can stay here. I've got a game to play.

STANLEY: A game?

TOM: And we haven't really talked. Did I tell you that I think you're kind of exciting?

STANLEY: Me?

TOM: Well, interesting but that's such a dull word.

STANLEY: *(It starts to rain.)*
Knew it would….rain's like lead pellets.

TOM: It's good for grass but who's got grass in the Bronx.

STANLEY: Our lawn in Queens turned yellow cause of the drought. Maybe it's a sun shower?

TOM: All those signs in the subway: Save water, every flush wastes 8 gallons. If I go to the bathroom twice in one day, I feel like a goddamn anarchist.

STANLEY: I hope it stops soon.

TOM: Will you leave it alone; it's going to do what it wants anyway.

STANLEY: Can't leave without getting my suit all wet.

TOM: Stop worrying; relax for a change.

STANLEY: Martha has my pencil. Always in there. All the time.

TOM: Likes to crawl into my bed as soon as I get out of it. It makes her feel better. And she's a bit insecure, if you know what I mean.

STANLEY: Oh, she's insecure!

TOM: Got a right to feel better; that's why I don't mind and I always buy her apples. Wouldn't you like to play that game with me now?

STANLEY: No.

TOM: You'll get something out of it; something you've been missing.
(He looks at his watch.)
Stop that. It's raining and you can't go any place. We'll play "Bubble-Lights."

STANLEY: Not something simple. Parcheesi? It makes sense and doesn't mean anything.

TOM: Not artistic. Stanley, I'm an intellectual and I play "Bubble-Lights."

STANLEY: It's pouring.

TOM: You put out the lights.
(Stanley closes the blinds and puts out the lights and Tom gets her shoebox full of candles and stuff.)
I'm building a magic circle.
(She arranges the candles as they were when the play began.)

STANLEY: I don't want to play.

TOM: Quiet. Anger will clog you mind . . . And I won't let you in my circle . . . You want to, don't you?

STANLEY: How should I know?

TOM: Sit down and close your eyes.

STANLEY: And open my mouth?

TOM: No, keep that closed.
(Stanley sits and Tom lights all the candles.)
Stanley and Tom are sitting inside the Magic Circle. Open your eyes to a new thing . . . Nothing can harm us.

STANLEY: *(To himself, almost.)* Nothing was going to.

TOM: Silly . . . Everything was, inside a Magic Circle nothing can; otherwise it isn't a Magic Circle.

STANLEY: I've got to get out of here.

TOM: Stay and sit with Tom. Staying is part of the game. And if you leave your suit will get all soggy.

STANLEY: I don't know you. You do funny things to me. Sometimes, I just feel so good . . .

TOM: Stop it Stanley. I'm glad of what I am. So's Martha. We're just bitches and don't believe anything else. People know what we're about and nobody tries to sucker us for sentiment. You're the problem if there is one.

STANLEY: I am?

TOM: Different with that smile. Get mad and want to cut right out but you don't because your suit will get all sick or something. Or maybe you care; care too much and don't know any better. Like squirrels.

STANLEY: But I want to leave. But here I am staying.

TOM: I'm a Scorpio.

STANLEY: And what's Martha? I haven't even seen her.

TOM: Time for the bubbles. We're going to blow that over the lights.

STANLEY: They'll burst; that's physics.

TOM: Forget it, there's more to Bubble-Lights than Isaac Newton. You've got to get them as near the flame as you can, without breaking them.

STANLEY: How does anybody win?

TOM: Don't understand yet. It's as if you were racing your shadow, the best you can do is switch the light to give you an advantage…you learn from this game.
(She begins to use a bubble-pipe and blow bubbles near the flames. She goes from flame to flame. Stanley doesn't move.)
Stanley, it's not that complicated.
(As she blows.)
Snickers-Flickers; Tears-Jeers . . .

STANLEY: Snicker-Flicker; Flicker-snicker. What am I doing?

TOM: Try. Doesn't take much guts. And after the game, when it's absolutely over, you won't be afraid any more.
(Stanley tries but not very hard.)
Light, light shine on my bubbles; might, might, let them through without much trouble....Stanley, you're breaking them.

STANLEY: I don't think I give a damn. That's it, not a damn. What do I care if some bubble gets burned or not? Silly game, silly problem.

TOM: We've got to finish now.

STANLEY: *(Rising.)* It's over.

TOM: Not until we put out the light. With your fingers.... Did you ever hold a match to your finger to see how much you can take?

STANLEY: I burnt myself.

TOM: Well, I burn myself all the time but I can take a lot more now....Putting out the candle takes some guts, Stanley.

STANLEY: Don't worry about mine.
(They each do a candle, putting it out with their fingers.)

TOM: No burn.

STANLEY: *(Feeling some pain.)*

No burn.
(They do the next candle together. Both saying, "No burn.")

TOM: Almost done. The first time done perfectly. I knew it could happen.
(As they begin to do the last candle each an Air Raid siren begins to howl.)
Not that now.

STANLEY: Burn . . . I've burnt myself.

TOM: Ah-h-h -h . . . Ruined it. Ruined again.

STANLEY: *(Goes to the window and opens the blinds. A cloudy sky lights the room.)*
Still raining out there. Maybe it'll be a sun-shower; something quick. Tom, I've burnt myself. I'm not a sheet of asbestos.

TOM: It's ruined….And that siren.

STANLEY: Just a siren.

TOM: Not just. It upsets Tom.

STANLEY: Come on….I'm going to get Herman.

TOM: What are you doing?

STANLEY: I'm going to go.

TOM: The big noise scares Tom.

STANLEY: Who can talk to you . . . It shouldn't scare you.

TOM: Why shouldn't it?

STANLEY: Happens all the time.

TOM: Should scare....How do you know it's not real this time? Maybe the bombs are coming and this time is different from all the others.
(She puts her thumb in her mouth.)

STANLEY: Got to get used to it.

TOM: And then live in Queens with convertibles.

STANLEY: I've adjusted to it.

TOM: You have?

STANLEY: Doesn't concern me. Understand. You can't worry about everything and let it upset you.

TOM: But if it's real, then you'd care.

STANLEY: Then what's the use? What the hell's the use?

TOM: Still going on. Isn't it too long? I mean if it's only a drill or a test?

STANLEY: They always seem long….Hey, the rain's starting to stop.

TOM: But the siren hasn't.

STANLEY: Now there's nothing to….Except Martha. I'd like to see her.

TOM: Stanley stay with Tom until the siren stops.

STANLEY: *(Now aware of the siren.)*
Yes….Hey, no that's being stupid….just another drill.

TOM: They're run by the people outside. Who can tell? People outside run anything; ruin everything. I'm, I'm scared.

STANLEY: I always used to think that, about it, but you grow out of it.

TOM: It's too long.

STANLEY: Well, it hasn't stopped….what's the matter….And the rain has. Rather hear the rain.

TOM: *(Racing to the door.)*
She's been listening at the door.
(To Martha)
No!
(Tom locks the bedroom door.)

TOM: She wants you to stay with her. No, Martha, Stanley stays here.

STANLEY: I've never even seen Martha.

TOM: Listen....screeching....a strangled cat.

STANLEY: I hate the sound. What about Martha in there?

TOM: You can't go. Got to stay here with me.

STANLEY: Is she really in there?

TOM: Tom wants Stanley. While there's still time.

STANLEY: I've got to go.

TOM: But the siren.

STANLEY: There's no one in there.
(To the siren.)
Please stop, stop....please.

TOM: Come lie with me.

STANLEY: I'm tired of being scared....And the door's not locked.

TOM: It doesn't matter.

STANLEY: There's no Martha!

TOM: *(To Stanley.)* Relax your nerves. Smile, will ya.

STANLEY: I'm scared.

TOM: *(As she pulls him down to the sofa.* Sh-h-h-h dear, come to Scorpio.

(THE LIGHTS FADE OUT AS THE SIREN CONTINUES TO HOWL.)

THE END

ABOUT THE AUTHOR

Seth Alan Barkas (1945-1969) grew up in Bayside, Queens, New York City. He graduated from Public School 31, Junior High School 74, and Bayside High School, where he ran for class president and was given an award by the Kiwanis Club for his service to the community.

At New York University, Seth majored in drama. An honors student, he was Feature Editor of the student newspaper, *Heights Daily News*. He developed a column, "Slightseeing," where he listed free or low-cost activities in New York City.

After graduation, following a brief time at the Iowa Writing Program, he became a TV news reporter/producer at WBAL-TV News in Baltimore, Maryland. He covered the civil rights and peace activities beats. He also started a film company, Cine Alliance, to make commercials and feature films.

A year later, he and his family relocated to Forest Hills, New York City. Seth worked as an editor at Prentice-Hall before beginning a fulltime freelance writing career. At the time of his death, he was a freelance movie critic for *Baltimore* magazine and a freelance theatre critic for *Show Business* newspaper. He was reviewing an off-off-Broadway play the night he was stabbed by a gang; he died several days later.

Here, reprinted with permission, is the tribute that ran along with Seth's last movie review, published posthumously in the March 1969 issue of *Baltimore* magazine:

SETH A. BARKAS

Seth Barkas is dead at 23, the victim of a moronic gang attack on a New York Street. What sickening commentary on our time, what irony: Barkas, as readers of his column know, abhorred the cheap, gloating violence which permeates so many American films, and he used his voice against it.

"I always cry at movies," he once confessed to us. "Me, a critic. My wife just shakes her head." That tells a lot about Seth Barkas: the compassion he felt for people was close to the surface, and it showed, with no pretenses, in his work. He wanted very much to do something about the lack of meaningful films for children and he was just beginning to emerge an important spokesman in the cause. His recent letter in the *New York Times* on the topic was, in our opinion, something of a masterpiece.

We enjoyed watching the work of this gentle young man develop, and it was developing rapidly. He did not have time to really take his place in the world, or leave his mark upon it. But he was going to, we were all sure of that.

The Seth Barkas Memorial Prize in Creative Writing, established in 1969 at his alma mater, New York University, is awarded annually. (Contributions in his honor may be sent to: Seth Barkas Memorial Prize in Creative Writing, New York University, College of Arts and Sciences, 100 Washington Square East, Room 909A, Main Building, New York, New York 10003.)

www.ingramcontent.com/pod-product-compliance
Lightning Source LLC
Chambersburg PA
CBHW031258090426
42742CB00007B/503

* 9 7 8 1 8 8 9 2 6 2 5 1 2 *